BMW Z3 and Z4
The Complete Story

OTHER TITLES IN THE CROWOOD AUTOCLASSICS SERIES

ALFA ROMEO 105 SERIES SPIDER
ALFA ROMEO 916 GTV AND SPIDER
ALFA ROMEO 2000 AND 2600
ALFA ROMEO SPIDER
ASTON MARTIN DB4, DB5 & DB6
ASTON MARTIN DB7
ASTON MARTIN V8
AUSTIN HEALEY 100 & 3000 SERIES
BMW M3
BMW M5
BMW CLASSIC COUPÉS 1965–1989
BMW Z3 AND Z4
CITROEN DS SERIES
CLASSIC JAGUAR XK
FERRARI 308, 328 & 348
FORD CONSUL, ZEPHYR AND ZODIAC
FROGEYE SPRITE
GINETTA ROAD AND TRACK CARS
JAGUAR E-TYPE
JAGUAR F-TYPE
JAGUAR MKS 1 AND 2, S-TYPE AND 420
JAGUAR XJ-S
JAGUAR XK8
JENSEN V8
JOWETT JAVELIN AND JUPITER
LAMBORGHINI COUNTACH
LAND ROVER DEFENDER
LAND ROVER DISCOVERY
LAND ROVER FREELANDER
MGA
MGB
MGF AND TF
MAZDA MX-5
MERCEDES-BENZ 'FINTAIL' MODELS
MERCEDES-BENZ S-CLASS

MERCEDES-BENZ W113
MERCEDES-BENZ W123
MERCEDES-BENZ W124
MERCEDES-BENZ W126
MERCEDES W201 (190) SERIES
MERCEDES SL SERIES
MERCEDES SL & SLC 107 SERIES
MORGAN 4/4: THE FIRST 75 YEARS
PEUGEOT 205
PORSCHE 924/928/944/968
PORSCHE AIR-COOLED TURBOS
PORSCHE BOXSTER AND CAYMAN
PORSCHE CARRERA: THE AIR-COOLED ERA
PORSCHE CARRERA: THE WATER-COOLED ERA
PORSCHE WATER-COOLED TURBOS
RANGE ROVER: THE FIRST GENERATION
RANGE ROVER: THE SECOND GENERATION
RANGE ROVER SPORT
RELIANT THREE-WHEELERS
ROVER 75 AND MG ZT
ROVER 800
ROVER P4
ROVER P6
ROVER SD1
SAAB 99 & 900
SHELBY AND AC COBRA
SUBARU IMPREZA WRX AND WRX STI
SUNBEAM ALPINE & TIGER
TOYOTA MR2
TRIUMPH SPITFIRE & GT6
TRIUMPH TR6
TRIUMPH TR7
VW KARMANN GHIAS AND CABRIOLETS
VOLVO 1800
VOLVO AMAZON

BMW Z3 and Z4

The Complete Story

James Taylor

THE CROWOOD PRESS

First published in 2017 by
The Crowood Press Ltd
Ramsbury, Marlborough
Wiltshire SN8 2HR

enquiries@crowood.com

www.crowood.com

This impression 2020

© James Taylor 2017

All rights reserved. No part of this publication may be reproduced or transmitted in any form or by any means, electronic or mechanical, including photocopy, recording, or any information storage and retrieval system, without permission in writing from the publishers.

British Library Cataloguing-in-Publication Data
A catalogue record for this book is available from the British Library.

ISBN 978 1 78500 276 2

Designed and typeset by Guy Croton Publishing Services, Tonbridge, Kent

Printed and bound in India by Parksons Graphics

CONTENTS

	Introduction and Acknowledgements	6
CHAPTER 1	A SPORTING HERITAGE	7
CHAPTER 2	THE Z3, 1995–1999	22
CHAPTER 3	THE Z3, 2000–2002	50
CHAPTER 4	THE M DIVISION'S Z3	70
CHAPTER 5	THE E85 Z4, 2002–2005	88
CHAPTER 6	MAKEOVER – THE 2006–2008 MODELS	108
CHAPTER 7	THE M DIVISION'S Z4	126
CHAPTER 8	THE SECOND GENERATION Z4 – THE E89 MODELS	144
CHAPTER 9	A Z3 AND Z4 BUYER'S GUIDE	172
	Index	191

INTRODUCTION AND ACKNOWLEDGEMENTS

Two-seat sports cars, especially roofless ones, were out of fashion when BMW was becoming firmly established as a maker of cars with dynamic driving qualities in the late 1960s and early 1970s. Car makers everywhere were afraid that US legislation would outlaw the sale of such cars on safety grounds, and BMW wisely held back. By the time the threat of that legislation had receded, the company had sealed its reputation as a maker of closed cars with sporting qualities.

So BMW was late in getting back into a market sector where its products had been prominent during the 1930s. The low-volume Z1 of 1988 made clear that the company was thinking about an open two-seater, but it was not until 1995 brought the Z3 that the BMW sports car in 'affordable' form reappeared. Since then, the company has never looked back: the 2002 E85 Z4 and 2009 E89 Z4 continued where the Z3 had left off, refining the roadster concept and making of it something that was once again central to the BMW image.

I have been interested in the BMW roadsters since the early days of the Z3, and have also followed BMW the company closely over two and a half decades or more. So it has been a pleasure to write this history of the roadsters' rebirth – and that of the coupé alternatives that accompanied the Z3 and first-generation Z4.

I need to make one small point about the format of this book. You will see that I have devoted far more pages to the Z3 and first-generation Z4 models than to the second-generation Z4. This is deliberate: at the time of writing there was greater enthusiast interest in the earlier cars, and I felt they therefore deserved the lion's share of a book like this. There is already enthusiast interest in the E89 Z4s, and I don't doubt that will increase as the cars become older and more affordable. In the meantime, please treat the chapter about them as a placeholder: if this book goes to a second edition, then will perhaps be the time to go into more detail to meet enthusiast expectations.

As always, credit needs to be given where credit is due. BMW (GB) and the BMW Global Media Service have between them been enormously helpful in providing the basic material for this book. Special thanks go to Ian, Barbara and Melanie at Brooklands Books for giving me access to so many road tests in their vast library. Various individual enthusiasts have chipped in with pieces of extra information, and so have several websites and online forums. Many thanks to all of them and, as always, only I can be blamed for any mistakes in understanding what they told me.

James Taylor
Oxfordshire
June 2016

CHAPTER ONE

A SPORTING HERITAGE

As a much-admired builder of sporting machinery, BMW was in an extraordinary position for most of the 1980s. For the German car maker had no traditional sports car in its model range. Nobody doubted the performance and handling qualities of its top models, and nobody doubted the excellence of its engines, but there was no open two-seater available with the blue-and-white roundel badge.

The reasons for this were many and varied. Perhaps most important of all was that by the 1980s BMW had only just pulled off an astonishing recovery from near-extinction at the start of the 1960s, and that building such frivolities as a sports car had been put on the back-burner until the company was back on a sound commercial footing. And yet without a sporting undertone to the products of its revival, BMW would have found those years of recovery much more difficult. Competing in a German domestic market dominated by the solid and superbly engineered cars of Mercedes-Benz, and where the lower-priced sector was well catered for by the likes of Opel, Ford and Volkswagen, BMW had to be different. That sporting undertone was what made it different.

Although there was probably an element of calculation about distinguishing itself from rival manufacturers in this way, it was certainly not an idea that had been picked out of the blue. In earlier years, BMW had enjoyed a reputation as a builder of sporting machinery that had included traditional open two-seater models. In fact, it was cars like this that had made its reputation in the first place.

In the Beginning

BMW's early years had been spent as a maker of aero engines, and the company's name actually reflected its beginning in that industry. The letters BMW came from Bayerische Motoren Werke ('Bavarian Engine Works'), and from 1916 the company had focused on building some of the best aero engines around. However, the opportunities to sell those engines became rather more limited during the 1920s when Germany was caught in the grip of rampant inflation and reconstruction of its military powers was severely restricted by the humiliating Treaty of Versailles that the country had been forced to sign in 1919. So BMW began to look around for additional ways of deploying its talents and its factory space.

One industry that was booming in the 1920s was that of the motor car. Everywhere that cars were being made, synergies were being discovered between the design and manufacture of cars and aeroplanes, and it made sense for BMW to look at the possibility of moving into the car industry. The opportunity arose in October 1928 when the small German car maker Dixi, based at Eisenach, ran into financial difficulties. BMW did not hesitate and bought it out and, for the first few months, continued to run the company under its original name as a subsidiary.

At this stage, Dixi was best known for building a version of the British Austin Seven under licence. The Austin Seven had been carefully designed to offer the minimum of everything that was needed in a car, in order to keep its price low and attractive, but it had also been designed to offer more than the ultra-cheap cyclecars of the time. The formula was an attractive one, and was eminently suitable for a Germany where economic circumstances were difficult. So Dixi took on manufacture of the Austin design in 1927, adding a few features of its own to give the car extra appeal to German buyers.

Once BMW had taken over, the Dixi name was dropped, and the upgraded 1929 models became known as BMW 3/15 models – the 3 was the 3PS taxable horsepower

■ A SPORTING HERITAGE

The 1931 3/15 DA2 model, derived from Britain's Austin Seven and with saloon bodywork by Ambi-Budd in Berlin, seems a far cry from the sleek BMWs that came to characterize the marque. Yet the sporting ambition was already present: the chassis was available with a two-seat roadster body as well.

rating and the 15 was the actual power output of 15PS (14.8bhp). During 1930 the original three-model range (saloon, convertible and delivery van) was expanded to include a sports roadster – BMW's first – with a drop-centre front axle to lower the car's centre of gravity and an 18PS (17.75bhp) version of the engine. Known as the Wartburg model (after a castle overlooking the town of Eisenach), it was withdrawn after just a year as the sports car market collapsed in the Great Depression. In 1932, the licence manufacturing agreement with Austin expired, and BMW chose not to renew it. By this time, they were ready with their own car designs.

As the BMW 3/20 appeared in 1933, the German economy was just beginning to look up under the leadership of the National Socialist Party. While ruthlessly suppressing political opposition and asserting German nationalism, the Nazi party did succeed in improving job prospects and reining in inflation. The building of new Autobahns provided an opportunity to create new touring cars and saloons, and BMW did exactly that alongside other new sports models such as the 315/1 of 1934.

The Roadsters of the 1930s

The 315/1 – presented at the Berlin Motor Show in May 1934 – was the first roadster engineered by BMW's own designers. Based on the chassis of the company's existing 315 saloon, it had a more steeply raked radiator, just two seats behind a low windscreen, a folding roof (really for weather emergencies only) and a tapered tail. To reduce wind resistance in the fashion of the times, its rear wheels were hidden under spats. Like the saloon newly introduced at the same show, it had a 1.5-litre 6-cylinder engine developed from the 1.2-litre type used in the earlier BMW 303, but in the sports car it had 40bhp as against the 34bhp in the saloon, and in production form that sports car was capable of 75mph (120km/h).

The 315/1 quickly established its sporting credentials with success in the 1934 International Alpine Rally, run between Nice and Munich over a distance of 2,867km (1,781 miles). One of the five works-entered cars finished first in its category, and all five completed the rally without incurring any penalty points at all. Over the next couple

A SPORTING HERITAGE

The 1934 315 (not to be confused with the earlier 3/15 model) was designed by **BMW** engineers and was made available with this attractive roadster bodywork.

BMW campaigned the cars itself, well aware of the value of sporting success in impressing a car's qualities on the buying public. These are 315/1 roadsters at the 1934 '2,000km across Germany' race, in which BMW won a gold medal.

■ A SPORTING HERITAGE

of years, the little BMW became a serious contender in motor sport events, driven by both works and private drivers, and a 'special' built by Ralph Roese was still winning races in 1939, when Roese carried off the German Road Racing Championship. Meanwhile, BMW had capitalized on the car's success by making a more powerful version available – this time with a 1.9-litre engine tuned to 55bhp. Called the 319/1 and available between 1934 and 1936, the car was another success in competition, although its high retail price kept sales relatively low.

Other manufacturers made strenuous efforts to outdo the BMW roadsters in the mid-1930s, and the company could not afford to rest on its laurels. Further engine development found higher outputs within the capacity constraints of the 2-litre class, and from summer 1936 BMW had another new contender. This was the BMW 328, whose new 2-litre engine would be used not only for the sports car but also to power BMW's larger road cars, both saloons and grand touring cabriolets. In overall charge of the 328's development was Fritz Fiedler, and there were significant contributions from Alex von Falkenhausen and Ernst Loof, who would later play important parts in the history of BMW after the Second World War.

The 328 was introduced as a specialist sports-racing machine at the Eifelrennen race in June 1936, where it won the 2-litre class. The model became available as a road machine as well and during 1937 achieved more than 100 class wins in competition. In 1938 it won its class at Le Mans and won the RAC Tourist Trophy, the Alpine Rally and the Mille Miglia, following that in 1939 by another RAC Rally win and a class first (plus fifth overall) at Le Mans. A special works coupé won the 1940 Mille Miglia at an average speed of 103.6mph (166.7km/h), but by that time war had broken out and many potential competitors stayed away from the Italian event.

Much in the same mould as the 315/1 but far more powerful and modern in concept was the BMW 328 roadster of 1936. The wheel spats helped link the design back to the earlier 315 but were usually removed for sporting events to speed wheel changing.

A SPORTING HERITAGE

The 328 roadster became a competition favourite. Here, a clutch of examples contest an event held in the City Park at Hamburg during 1939.

The 2-litre BMW engine was used in the elegant 327/28 coupé – a 327 model of the late 1930s fitted with the higher-powered engine of the 328 roadster.

■ A SPORTING HERITAGE

In the Doldrums

During the 1940s and 1950s, BMW was in very bad shape. At the end of the Second World War in 1945, the company had lost one of its major factories (at Eisenach) to the Russian-controlled eastern sector of the country, and for the next few years struggled to survive in the harsh postwar economic climate from its main factory in Munich. It restarted motorcycle production somewhat hesitantly in 1948 but built and dismissed a number of prototype cars over the next couple of years. Among these was a most attractive model that was clearly inspired by the little Fiat 500 and was thought for a time to be the sort of car that Germans – once again going through an extremely difficult economic period – might want to buy. In the meantime, many of its engineers had probably begun to despair of getting back into building proper sporting cars. Two of them had left the company to set up on their own as sports car builders.

One of them was Alex von Falkenhausen, who had been a key member of the design team responsible for the pre-war BMW 328. He set up AFM (Alex von Falkenhausen Motorenbau) to tune surviving examples of the cars, and from 1948 went on to build his own car around the 328's engine. AFM cars did well in German motor sport events and elsewhere in Europe over the next few years, and fitted into the Formula Two regulations under which the World Driver's Championship was run in 1952–53. However, as Formula Two faded away, von Falkenhausen decided to return to BMW, where from 1954 he became head of the company's racing division, a position he would retain for more than two decades.

The other was Ernst Loof, who had also worked on development of the 328 in the 1930s. Like von Falkenhausen, he set up in business to work on surviving examples of the cars, rebuilding them and tuning them for track use, and sending them out as BMW-Veritas models. Although sporting success came as early as 1947, BMW objected to the use of their name and later that year Loof began to badge his cars simply as Veritas. By 1949 Loof and his partners had developed a road-going version of their Veritas racer. They switched to a new 2-litre engine built by Heinkel but money was tight and the company had to suspend production in 1950. Later that year, Loof set up a new company, again building Veritas

Even a specially designed two-door coupé body (in this case by Baur) could not disguise the essentially heavy lines of the 502 models.

A SPORTING HERITAGE

Desperate times called for desperate measures, and BMW assembled the Isetta 'Bubble Car' under licence in the mid-1960s. The rotating amber beacon on this one was not a standard feature!

cars with the Heinkel engine, but the money ran out again. So Veritas was liquidated, its assets were bought by BMW, and Loof returned to the BMW fold, working in styling and body engineering until his early death in 1956.

The stories of these two BMW engineers show that the green shoots of sports and racing cars were sprouting at Munich during the 1950s and 1960s, and it could only be a matter of time before BMW returned to its 1930s roots. Yet the BMW products of the early 1950s would have given onlookers little hope that such a return was possible, for they were far from sporting in nature.

It was 1951 before BMW felt it had a car design that was right for the times, and 1952 before that car – the 501 – entered volume production. Germans had endured the austerity of the late 1940s and by the start of the new decade were beginning to reap the early benefits of the Wirtschaftswunder ('economic miracle') that would turn their country into a major force in Europe once again. They no longer wanted small and cheap cars that reminded them of the difficult years, although several companies continued to offer such types; what they wanted was large and luxurious models that reflected their new-found prosperity. The BMW 501 was one of those cars.

Big, sturdy and deliberately middle-class, the 501 and its derivatives reflected BMW styling themes of the 1930s, and as a result they dated rather quickly and gained the rather disdainful nickname of Barockengeln ('Baroque angels') because their bulbous and flowing lines reminded people of the carved wooden figures in south German and Austrian churches from the Baroque period of the seventeenth and early eighteenth centuries. Early models had a revived version of the pre-war BMW 2-litre 6-cylinder engine, but later ones took on a newly designed all-alloy V8 – and that would later take the company back into the two-seater sports car market, although it would be a short-lived and ultimately unsuccessful return.

Clearly aware that there was still a market for small and cheap cars in Germany, BMW aimed to broaden its range from 1955 by taking out a licence to build the Italian Isetta 'Bubble Car'. This could hardly have been more different from the 501 family, but it did make manufacturing sense to BMW at the time because it could use one of the company's own motorcycle engines. A sports car it was not, but sales of the little three-wheeler did help to keep BMW alive and did give it the confidence to develop its first post-war two-seater model.

13

■ A SPORTING HERITAGE

It would be some time before BMW entered the roadster market again after the end of the Second World War. This was a design for what eventually became the 507, produced in 1954 by Ernst Loof who had returned to BMW after closing his own Veritas sports car business. The Loof design was rejected in favour of one by Albrecht Goertz.

The BMW 507

The impetus for the design of the BMW 507 actually came from Max Hoffmann, who had developed a thriving business importing European cars into the USA. BMW had no car they could really offer him, but they did pick up on his assertion that he could sell a high-performance sports car in large quantities if they could build one. Such a car would only be feasible if it could use elements of other production BMWs, of course, and that immediately steered minds towards the company's latest V8 engine and its associated powertrain components.

During 1954, the newly returned Ernst Loof was given the job of designing and building a prototype BMW roadster on the 501-derived 502 chassis with the company's latest 2.6-litre V8 engine. In the meantime, Max Hoffmann suggested to a US-based German car designer of his acquaintance that BMW might welcome a new sports car design. That designer, Albrecht von Goertz, contacted BMW and produced not only a sports roadster design but also a grand touring coupé design. The Goertz sports car design won the day against the Loof design and became the BMW 507, while his grand tourer entered production as the BMW 503.

Goertz's curvaceous roadster with its optional demountable hardtop had a shape that has worn incredibly well over the years. By the time it entered production in 1956, BMW had a larger and more powerful version of their V8 engine ready, and the 507 came as standard with a 3.2-litre engine that developed 150bhp in initial twin-carburettor form and was later uprated to 165bhp with a triple-carburettor installation. However, the 507 had barely become established before it was faced with serious opposition from the Mercedes-Benz 300SL, which from 1957 became available as a roadster after three years in production as a gullwing-door coupé.

A SPORTING HERITAGE

The Goertz design for the 507 was quite stunning, although the car was too expensive to sell strongly and faced serious competition from the Mercedes-Benz 300SL.

The 507 could also be had with a hardtop, as on this example pictured at Munich airport. This car also has the optional centre-lock wheels.

Despite its relative rarity, the V8-engined 507 remains well regarded and is a highly prized classic today.

A SPORTING HERITAGE

In the 1950s, one of BMW's main aims was to establish a reputation for itself in the USA as a maker of sporting cars. Like the 507, the 503 had a V8 engine and was designed by Goertz, but this cabriolet was more of a grand tourer than a roadster.

The competition with the already-legendary Mercedes was one reason why the 507 never became a strong seller. Another was cost, and a third was that BMW took its time to get production under way. Although the car had been announced at the Frankfurt Motor Show in autumn 1955, the first cars were not delivered until the following year. Customers complained of a lack of boot space in the first cars, and so BMW made a smaller tank available as an option – which made refuelling stops necessary more frequently if the car was used as intended. So just 254 507s were sold in three years of production, all with left-hand drive. The experience left BMW not very keen to try its hand at another sports roadster.

Crisis and Renewal

Meanwhile, BMW's small-car designs had gradually been growing in confidence and ability. The 600 of 1957 drew on the company's Isetta experience but added a larger motorcycle engine to a four-wheel design, and the 700 of 1959 once again used a motorcycle engine, this time in a larger body with attractive lines penned by Italian designer Giovanni Michelotti. Over the six years of its production, the car became BMW's bestseller since 1945, and more than 188,000 examples were built. But it arrived too late to stave off a financial crisis that threatened to engulf the company in 1960.

By the end of 1959, BMW was in trouble, having lost DM15 million on that year's turnover of DM150 million. A general meeting of shareholders in December strongly supported a proposal from the bank – BMW's chief creditor – that the company should sell out. Mercedes' parent company, Daimler-Benz, in buoyant financial health, circled expectantly.

However, a substantial minority of shareholders blocked the proposal and put forward a counter-proposal to find another source of funding that would enable BMW to remain independent. Over the next two months, two businessmen who already owned a substantial proportion of BMW shares began to increase their holdings. By the autumn of 1960, some two-thirds of BMW shares belonged to the brothers Harald and Herbert Quandt, and BMW once again had funds.

Next, it needed direction. BMW's board wisely decided that the company should proceed with its plan to enter the medium-sized saloon market, but that work done on such a car during the 1950s should be halted and the designers should think again. They did, and the new car that was shown in prototype form at the 1961 Frankfurt Motor Show embodied the best of what BMW could achieve. Not only was it attractively styled, with modern unitary construction

A SPORTING HERITAGE

The Neue Klasse of 1961 was the car that hauled BMW out of the doldrums, and the company has never looked back. As a medium-sized saloon with sporting qualities, it gave the company an enduring image that remains in place today – and BMW's Z3 and Z4 roadsters would always to some extent have to fight against that image.

and a modern suspension layout, but it also had an engine derived from earlier proposals by Alex von Falkenhausen. That engine was designed with built-in 'stretchability' that would enable BMW to produce a variety of different sizes from the same basic design, and after the BMW 1500 entered production in 1962 it rapidly gained praise from professionals and customers alike. Its basic design kept the car and its derivatives in production right through until 1976 – and the engine design remained in production even beyond that.

Most important was that the BMW 1500 family of cars embodied the enthusiasm of designers who were determined to produce a sporting car. It was not yet a traditional sports two-seater because its role was to re-establish BMW as a mainstream car manufacturer, but it embodied the essential elements of a sporting car in its performance and handling. It also made clear that BMW was back and that its sporting heritage remained intact. During the 1970s, the successors of the 1500 range – the 5 Series four-door saloons and the 3 Series two-doors that replaced the '02' range of two-door cars derived from the 1500 – kept alive that sporting heritage and built on it. By 1980, everybody knew once again what BMW stood for.

The Wrong Time

In the 1960s, 'sports' meant high-performance saloons at BMW. This advertisement commemorates a 1964 victory by the 1800TI model.

But this was not yet the time to introduce a sports roadster again. There is not even any evidence to suggest that BMW considered such a project. Few car companies had such a model in their ranges at the start of the 1980s. Most of them

■ A SPORTING HERITAGE

This 1987 M3 cabriolet was what BMW was really all about in the 1980s. The M3 was the Motorsport-developed version of the 3 Series compact saloon, and the cabriolet version seen here was introduced almost reluctantly: BMW had become firmly wedded to tin-top models.

In the 1970s, BMW's sporting ambitions were tied to its big 6-cylinder coupés, which eventually tranformed into the formidable 'Batmobile' track cars.

A SPORTING HERITAGE

had fought shy of investing in any sort of open car when the 1970s had brought the threat of US legislation that would ban open cars on safety grounds. The issue was not just that the USA probably absorbed more open cars than any other country in the world; it was that other countries were likely to follow the lead of US legislators and also ban open cars. So the car makers gradually pensioned off their open models and did not replace them directly. In Britain, for example, the Triumph TR6 sports car was replaced by a firmly closed TR7 fixed-head coupé in 1975 – and it was some years before the car could be redeveloped as a convertible once the threat of that US legislation had receded.

At BMW, there were nevertheless a few open cars, at least of a kind. Playing for safety, the company had developed open-air versions of its 02 Series saloons in the 1970s and the 3 Series saloons that followed them. But these were not traditional convertibles; they were 'targa-top' models, constructed for BMW by the Baur coachworks and featuring a removable roof section that fitted between strong windscreen and rear upper body sections. That was as far as the company was prepared to go for the time being.

Things began to change in the early 1980s. The first evidence of a new approach at BMW was the introduction in 1986 of a proper cabriolet version of the E30 3 Series. Meanwhile, behind closed doors, the company had already begun to develop a two-seat roadster, the job of doing so having been handed to the future-products specialists at BMW Technik GmbH.

The BMW Z1

This car would become the first product of BMW Technik, and would arrive in 1987 as the BMW Z1. The Z was the initial letter of the word Zukunft – German for 'future' – and the car had been designed to a very loose brief that called for a two-seat sports roadster that would revitalize BMW's image and demonstrate that the company remained a leader in innovation and excitement. As the details of the design had been left to the BMW Technik engineers, it was hardly surprising that the Z1 ended up being something of an engineer's delight. It had a remarkable base-unit construction

Trying to shake off that 'tin-top' image, BMW drew on its other strength – advanced technology – to produce the Z1 roadster of 1988. There was perhaps too much technology for the car to be affordable, but BMW learned a lot from building and marketing the Z1.

■ A SPORTING HERITAGE

Even as late as 1999, BMW showed that it was more comfortable with large and powerful sports cars. This picture shows the Z8 roadster – a hugely expensive machine with a 4.9-litre V8 engine – next to its spiritual forebear, the 507 of the 1950s. The car had been previewed as a concept called the Z07 in 1997. By this time, of course, the Z3 was already on sale and gaining BMW a new reputation as a maker of affordable roadsters.

with demountable plastic skin panels, doors that dropped into the massive side sills, and a fully disappearing soft top.

Although the Z1 was a quite remarkable demonstration of BMW's abilities, it was not by any means an affordable or traditional sports roadster. BMW decided against farming out construction to a company such as Baur or Karmann, and chose to build the car in-house. Space constraints meant that production would have to be limited, and limited production inevitably raises the manufacturing cost of a car. One result was that there would be no Z1s with right-hand drive. Another was that the Z1's showroom price was simply forbidding. When it went on sale in the UK, it cost an eye-watering £26,500; back in 1986, BMW had optimistically hinted at a price of around £15,000.

While the Z1 was doing its job of demonstrating BMW's advanced technical skills, over in Japan the Mazda company was putting the finishing touches to a genuinely affordable two-seat roadster that it would bring to market in 1989. The Mazda MX-5 (it would be called the Miata in the USA) was a gamble for the company, which had never built a car of its type before. However, market research had made clear that the time was now right for such a car. There were thousands

A SPORTING HERITAGE

This press photograph released when the Z3 was announced was an attempt to resume BMW's roadster heritage. The Z3 in the foreground is almost certainly a pre-production model.

of customers who yearned for the sort of sports cars that the British Leyland companies – MG and Triumph – had made before production was stopped in 1981. The viability of those cars as everyday drivers was diminishing as they grew older, and owners wanted more modern replacements. Mazda even based many of the MX-5's features on those of British sports cars such as the MGB and the Lotus Elan.

The MX-5's massive success, particularly in the USA, certainly encouraged BMW to think about building their own affordable two-seat roadster. This would not be another Z1, but a genuine volume-production model with a price tag that made it accessible to the younger people who were most likely to want one. There could, of course, be more expensive versions with better equipment and higher performance as well, but the key factor was cost. By 1991, a brief had been passed down to the engineers at BMW Technik. That brief called for the design of an affordable two-seat roadster, and the implied benchmark was the Mazda MX-5.

But no BMW roadster yet had been in the 'affordable' category characterized by cars such as Britain's MGs and Triumphs or Italy's Fiats and Alfa Romeos. So even though the bottom end of the new roadster range might impinge on the territory opened up by the Mazda, BMW's vision for its new roadster was very much wider.

CHAPTER TWO

THE Z3, 1995–1999

As the 1980s opened, BMW was riding the crest of a huge wave of success. The company had already established itself on the global market with a series of highly successful saloon cars that were carefully designed to appeal to different types of customer. The compact 3 Series saloons were for young buyers and for older ones who wanted to downsize without compromising on quality; the medium-sized 5 Series cars were for family buyers; and the large 7 Series models were for those who needed a luxury saloon for prestige purposes. It was already clear that with careful management this model strategy could continue for a good many years, and that the engineering department would simply have to keep on improving each model range so that it kept ahead of rivals with the introduction of each successive generation.

That would keep the company ticking over profitably. However, if it was to expand and potentially make ever greater profits, it would need to develop new products for sectors of the car market where it was not yet represented. BMW management chose to establish a new future-products division to look at such products, and BMW Technik was set up as an umbrella organization for the company's research division and for the engineering teams who would be needed to take new product lines through to production. It has been described as an 'independent think tank' and would be quite separate from the mainstream engineers whose task was to keep existing products fresh and to develop their successors, although inevitably there would also have to be strong cooperative links between the two divisions.

The earliest Z3 in its entry-level form certainly lacked the glamour of some of the later models. This is an early 1.8-litre car, with the styled steel wheels characteristic of the model. With its soft top erected, the car looks compact and user-friendly; even the long bonnet is barely noticeable in this photograph.

THE Z3, 1995–1999

What a difference! This 4-cylinder car wears alloy wheels and is clearly being used for enjoyment, with the top down. The long bonnet and short rear deck are more evident here; like all the early cars, this one has no rollover bars behind the seats.

The US Factory

By the end of the 1980s, BMW was also giving due consideration to the question of manufacturing space. The Z1 experiment had highlighted the difficulties that would arise if the product portfolio was expanded without a corresponding expansion of manufacturing facilities. So the new roadster project became intimately bound up with the plan to expand BMW's manufacturing facilities.

It became clear early on that an additional factory in Germany was not the answer. One of the problems that BMW was facing by the early 1990s was that it was selling a very large proportion of its cars in North America (primarily the USA), and that each and every one of those cars had to be manufactured in Germany and then shipped across the Atlantic to the supplying dealer. The whole process took time and was expensive, and it was relatively inflexible as well. Worse, fluctuations in the exchange rate meant that profitability was sometimes affected by a factor completely beyond BMW's control.

BMW quickly focused on the idea of building an assembly plant in the USA. During 1992, they settled on a site at Greer, in South Carolina's Spartanburg County, and an official announcement was made on 22 June that year. The deal between BMW and the state government of South Carolina was an excellent one for both sides. South Carolina was very keen to attract more industry to provide work, and bought the greenfield site alongside Interstate 85 itself for $38 mil-

THE Z3, 1995–1999

The Spartanburg plant in South Carolina was home to Z3 assembly – and later to that of the first-generation Z4 as well.

lion. It then leased the site to BMW for a peppercorn rent of just $1 a year. This arrangement was to continue for thirty years; BMW could then choose to buy the land at market value or continue to rent it at the same favourable rate for a further twenty years, after which time it would be obliged to buy it at the going rate. The South Carolina government also agreed to fund the initial training of the start-up workforce of 570 employees under its special technical school scheme.

For BMW, the South Carolina site had multiple advantages. It had good road and rail links within the USA that would facilitate distribution of completed cars, and also excellent links to the deep-water port at Charleston, around 100 miles away on the Atlantic coast. An airport nearby would simplify travel for BMW executives visiting from Germany. Better yet: it would actually be cheaper to build cars there than in the BMW plants in Germany. At the time, the company quoted the average hourly wage of a Spartanburg employee with two years' experience as about $17,

which compared very favourably with his or her German equivalent who earned between $25 and $30. Offsetting this to some degree, however, was a much greater use of manual labour (as distinct from robots) at Spartanburg than in BMW's German plants. This may have been one of the conditions imposed by the South Carolina government.

Construction began on the Spartanburg site in April 1993 and construction of the main buildings was complete by January 1994. That month, the first members of the start-up workforce were hired, and an indication of the new factory's attraction for the local economy was that there had been more than 65,000 applicants for the 570 initial jobs. The factory was officially opened on 15 November 1994, although assembly of BMWs had in fact begun in early September.

The BMW plan was ambitious but carefully orchestrated. Beginning in June 1994, the Spartanburg logistics had been tested by bringing BMWs assembled in Germany for the US market in through the port of Charleston. The

The Z3's body-in-white comes down the lines at Spartanburg, early in the car's production life.

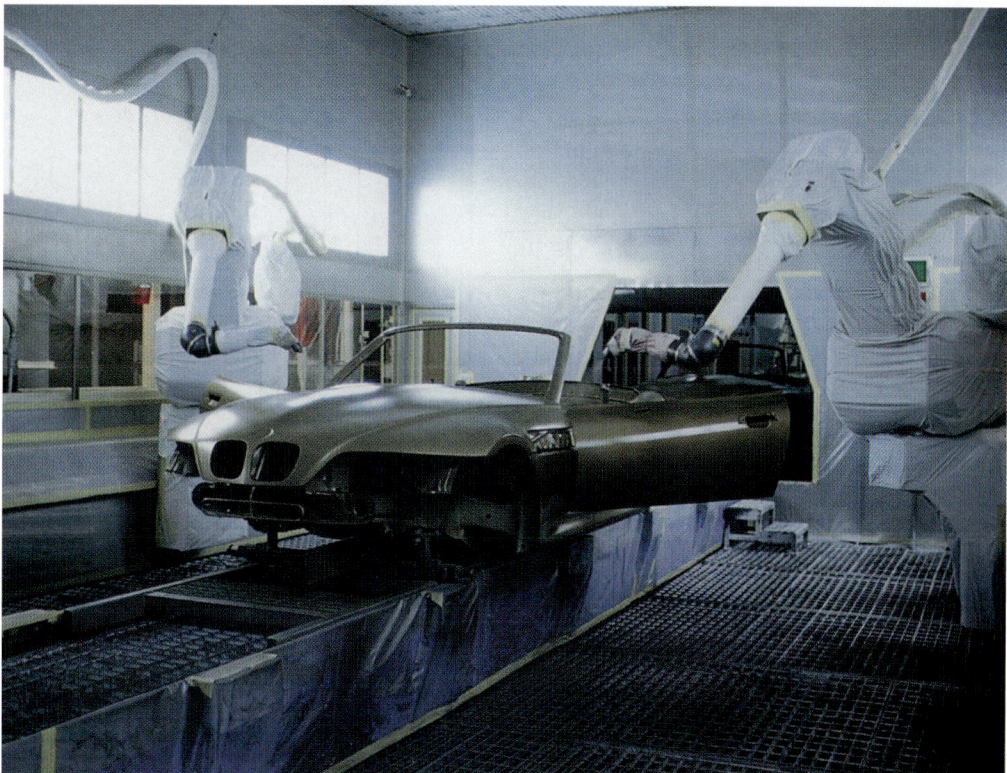

Z3 bodies were painted by a fully automatic system; the only human element was supervision of the robots.

THE Z3, 1995–1999

next stage of the plan was to assemble existing BMW models for the US market from CKD kits shipped in from Germany. The programme began with E36 318i saloons, added 318i coupés, and then in spring 1995 moved on to 328i saloons. However, the ultimate aim was to dedicate the US factory to the assembly of a single model range, and one that would not be built at any other BMW factory. Only the engines and transmissions would be shipped in from Germany. That single model range was the new two-seat roadster.

Human involvement again: a Z3 body on the assembly line at Spartanburg. Note the overhead conveyor that allowed the body to be positioned at a comfortable working height for the assembly-line staff.

The final line: a completed Z3 is seen here at the end of the assembly track at Spartanburg. Just visible is an example of the X5 Sports Activity Vehicle which was built on a separate assembly line at the plant from 1999.

Design and Development

Meanwhile, the new roadster was being designed and developed at BMW Technik. Inevitably, it would share existing or planned hardware with other BMW ranges in order to keep costs down. The most suitable hardware was that developed for the 3 Series models (which in the early 1990s were E36 types), and that probably explains why the new car took on the name of Z3. Logically, Z2 might have followed on from Z1, but the number three reinforced the link to the well-established and highly respected 3 Series.

BMW was already working on a derivative of the E36 3 Series for 1994 introduction that it called the Compact and was intended as its first foray into the hatchback market. This car had a special version of the E36's platform, where a short boot with a flat floor was made possible by ditching the standard E36 rear suspension in favour of the trailing-arm type from the older E30 3 Series models. With the wheelbase shortened from 2,700mm (106.30in) to 2,446mm (96.30in), this platform was also going to suit the requirements of the new Z3 and, largely as a result of this, the roadster was developed with the project code E36/7, which showed it was a derivative of the E36 saloon range.

The smallest engines then in production for the 3 Series were 4-cylinder types. There was a 1796cc engine in the 318i that had been introduced in 1987, and an 1895cc size was under development for introduction in the 1995 318iS. These would fit the bill for the affordable entry-level variants of the new roadster. If there were to be more expensive variants with bigger engines, these would have to use one or other of BMW's small-block 6-cylinders, and a good candidate was the 2.8-litre that would power the E36 328i from 1994. So the new car was designed around these engines and their associated gearboxes; although a five-speed manual would be the standard offering, BMW believed there would be demand for an automatic model as well and made preparations to offer an appropriate gearbox as an option.

All this was familiar hardware; it would be the body that would give the Z3 its unique character. So once the basic dimensions had been settled, work could begin on that. From the start there was never any question of such advanced designs as the Z1's base unit. Instead, there would be a welded steel bodyshell mounted directly to the E36-derived platform. Chris Bangle was the newly appointed head of BMW's design studio at the time, and it was a design proposal put forward by Joji Nagashima, the Tokyo-born

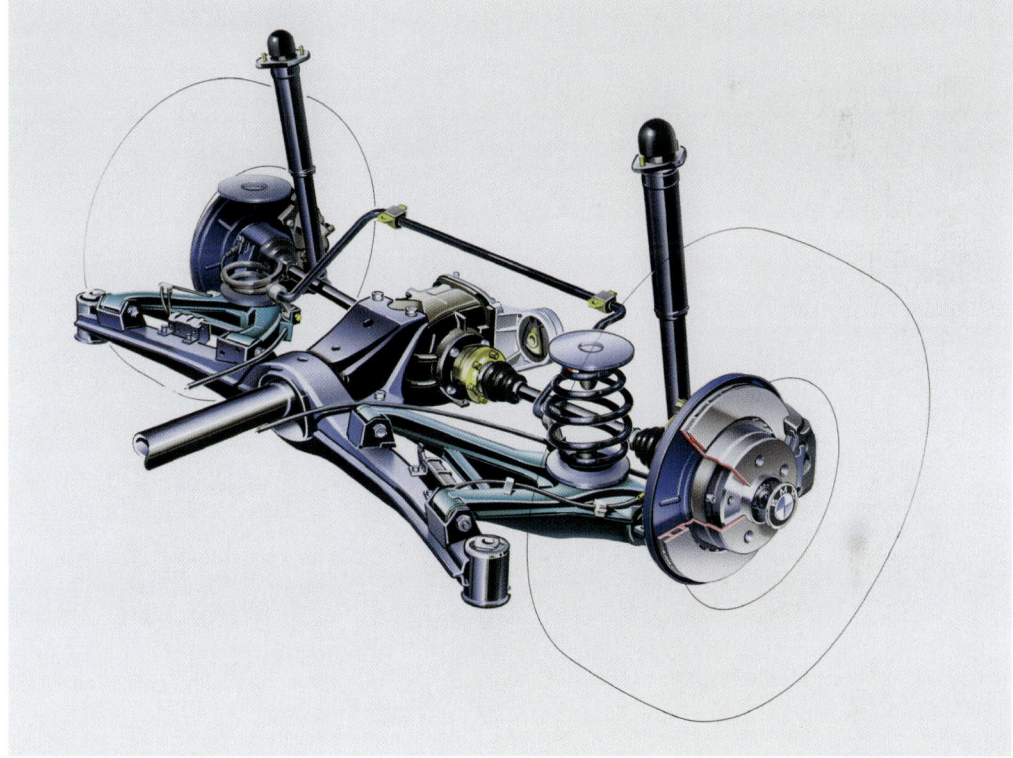

A flat boot floor was made possible by using the rear suspension of the E36 Compact models, but the decision was something of a compromise because it detracted from the Z3's handling.

■ THE Z3, 1995–1999

Many of the Z3's mechanical components came from the E36 3 Series cars, and in particular from the E36 Compact, which had an older style of rear suspension than the other models to suit its less spacious rear end.

This is the 1.8-litre engine in cutaway form. The camshaft was chain-driven and there were just two valves for each cylinder.

THE Z3, 1995–1999

Four-valve technology was becoming more common in the 1990s. This is the cylinder head of the M44 1.9-litre engine.

principal designer of the E36 models, that he selected in July 1992. From then on this was refined until the cut-off point in 1993 when everything had to be ready for the body tooling to be made.

Nagashima's design featured a long nose and short tail and incorporated the trademark twin-kidney grille within a wrap-around bonnet and a nose that resembled the one then being planned for the E39 5 Series saloons. Its flanks were given additional character by air vents on the front wings, a design feature inspired by BMW's own 507 roadster of the 1950s – although it must be said that nothing else from the 507 seems to have had a direct influence on the Z3 design.

The basic shape was passed to the production engineers, whose tasks included delivering structural rigidity and crashworthiness. In order to prevent the scuttle shake that so often affects open cars, they added bracing in critical areas such as the engine bay, between the floorpan and the bulkheads, and around the hood well. For good measure, they added a pair of elastically mounted anti-vibration weights inside the rear bumper housing, which were designed to

Overall responsibility for the shape of the Z3 fell to design chief **Chris Bangle**, whose later work for **BMW** would become quite controversial.

■ THE Z3, 1995–1999

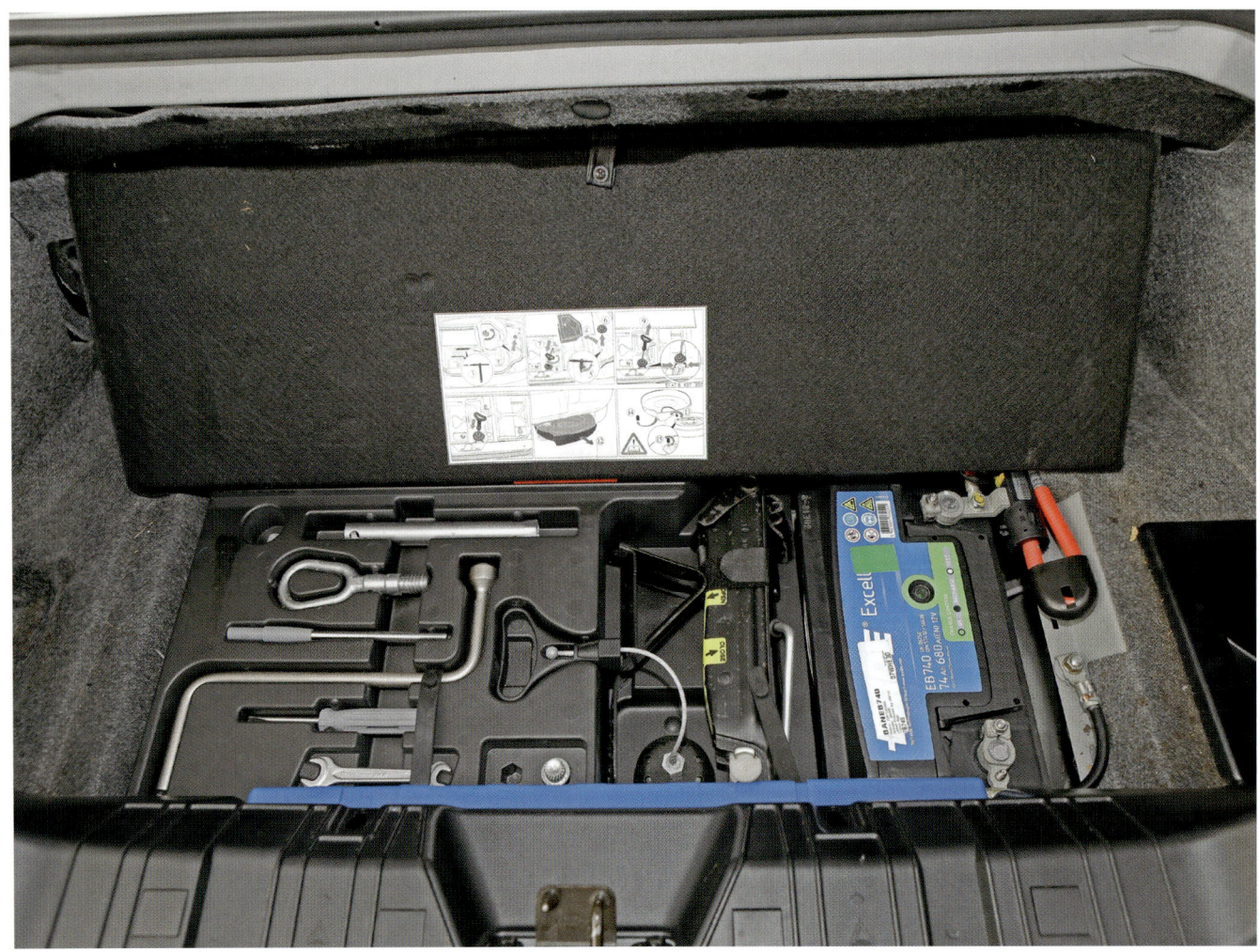

The battery was fitted in the boot to improve weight distribution. Note the neat tool tray, normally concealed below the boot flooring. MAGIC CAR PICS

move at a frequency that would compensate for any torsional vibration of the body. It was a determined effort but, as road testers would later complain, it was not enough to give the Z3 the rigidity it needed to ensure crisp handling.

A few compromises had to be made during the design process. The battery had to be located in the boot to improve weight distribution, but the trade-off was a loss of space in what was already a fairly small luggage compartment. There was certainly no room for a full-size spare wheel of even the smallest size planned for the car, and so a space-saver spare was tucked into a compartment in the boot floor. As an anti-theft measure, this was arranged so that it could only be opened from inside the boot and with the aid of a special tool.

There was less opportunity for compromise in the interior. Although the corporate parts bin could provide the instruments and the steering wheel with its airbag, almost everything else had to be specially designed. The dashboard was drawn up to allow for a passenger's side airbag, although this was planned as an extra-cost option for initial production models. Sweeping curves on its top surface and a rather attractive peaked instrument pod both added character and style to the design. Sadly, cost ruled out adding adjustment for the steering column.

Again using the MX-5 as a benchmark, BMW designed the interior to give more passenger room wherever they could, although in practice they could add no more than a few millimetres more than the Japanese car had. They made

THE Z3, 1995–1999

This was the car that the Z3 had to beat in the beginning – the Mazda MX-5, which reignited customer interest in affordable two-seat roadsters when it was introduced in 1989. This example is one of a rare special edition released in 1991; called the Le Mans 24 Hours, it celebrated Mazda's victory at the Le Mans event that year.

sure that there were plenty of stowage bins and pockets for oddments, and in particular designed a large lidded bin behind and between the seats.

The seats themselves were special, too, with integral head restraints and electric fore-and-aft adjustment as standard. The rake of the backrests, however, could not be changed; again, it would have added unacceptably to the cost. Cloth upholstery was planned for the basic models, with leather an extra-cost option. Then there was the soft top, designed to be an exemplary fit – one area where the features of traditional roadsters were no longer welcome – but cost again ruled out power assistance. The top was designed to disappear into a well behind the seats, where it could be covered by a leatherette tonneau cover held in place by stud fasteners. It featured a zip-out rear window for through ventilation when the top was up, and a novel feature was a mesh wind-blocker that could be erected behind the seats when the top was down to reduce wind buffeting at speed.

As the Wikipedia entry for the Z3 notes, design patents for the car were filed in Germany on 2 April 1994 and in the USA on 27 September 1994. The whole project – led, incidentally, by Dr Burkhard Göschel, who would later become BMW's overall R&D chief – had taken thirty-eight months from start to finish.

31

■ THE Z3, 1995–1999

The Launch

Everything came together as planned, and the media build-up for the Z3's launch began in the summer of 1995. BMW North America produced a video press release that was issued on 12 June 1995, and journalists elsewhere received press pictures of the new car in the late summer. Some of these certainly showed pre-production cars that had actually been hand-built in Germany, because the first Z3 did not come off the assembly line at Spartanburg until 20 September 1995. However, no cars would be released to the public for another five months. During this period, BMW ironed out quality-control problems and prepared the ground for the car's launch.

An important element in that preparation became clear in November. BMW had very cleverly managed to do a product-placement deal with the producers of the new James Bond 007 film *GoldenEye* which was released that month. The Z3 that appeared in it was of course a pre-production model – it had been so secret at the time of filming that it had been taken to and from the film studios in a closed box.

It was one of the very few prototype cars in existence, so BMW insisted that it should not be used for any chases or stunts. As a result, it appeared with Bond driving it during a scene supposedly shot in Cuba in which it was not driven with any special verve. Nevertheless, that was enough to whet the appetite of potential buyers and was certainly the first time many had ever seen a Z3.

Back in the real world, members of the motoring media were invited to a ride-and-drive event at the end of the year, and the Z3 was then formally introduced at the Detroit Motor Show in January 1996. The first deliveries to customers were made just a few weeks after that.

THE *GOLDENEYE* CAR

The prototype Z3 that featured in the James Bond film *GoldenEye* was painted in the production colour of Atlanta Blue. It also (notionally, at least) had a number of special features about which Bond was briefed by Q. There were Stinger missiles hidden behind the headlights, an emergency parachute braking system and a radar scanner in the form of an LCD screen in the dashboard. For good measure, the car also had a passenger ejector seat and a self-destruct system.

That same car was later put on permanent display in BMW's Zentrum museum at the Spartanburg assembly plant.

LEFT: Shrewd marketing: although the Z3 played only a very small part in the James Bond film *GoldenEye*, it was a masterpiece of product placement and gained priceless publicity for the new car. The blue Z3 can just be seen on this poster advertising the film.

The First Cars

All the first Z3s were 4-cylinder models, but there were different types for different markets. Some markets took the 114bhp 1.8-litre model, while others received only the 140bhp 1.9-litre derivative. A few markets, including Germany, had both.

The 1.8-litre car was not made available in either the UK or the USA, probably because both would have needed special features (right-hand drive for the UK and a special engine tune for the USA) that would have added to the cost. This least powerful variant was probably not expected to have much appeal in either country, and so there was a weak business case for building the special variants needed.

The entry-level car had a fairly basic specification. It came with 15in steel wheels, a five-speed gearbox, a single airbag, cloth upholstery and a choice of solid paint colours only. That meant there was a long options list. ABS, an automatic gearbox, a sports suspension that lowered the car by 15mm (0.6in), a 25 per cent limited-slip differential and alloy wheels in 16in and 17in sizes with appropriately sized tyres all cost extra. So did a passenger's airbag, air conditioning, leather upholstery and metallic paint finishes.

The 1.9-litre car, made available for both UK and US markets, was a much more attractive proposition. Strangely, perhaps, there were no badges to distinguish it from its smaller-engined sibling, and standard equipment levels were not particularly impressive even though ABS was fitted for all markets and metallic paints were available. Cars for the USA came with alloy wheels and electrically adjustable door mirrors as standard but still only one airbag. The US cars (and those for Japan) also had a square rear licence-plate holder. Traction control, air conditioning and (in most countries) leather upholstery were all extra-cost items.

Right-hand-drive cars were late in arriving. Although BMW in the UK had been accepting orders for Z3s since July 1995 against an anticipated on-sale date of September 1996, it would actually be March 1997 before the first cars arrived. Production had not begun until January. One reason suggested at the time was quality-control problems at the Spartanburg plant, but this has never been verified. Faced with disappointed customers, BMW GB offered those who had ordered a Z3 the option of preferential financing on a 318i convertible, with a guaranteed buy-back when their Z3s arrived. It seems that around 20 per cent of the 3,300 customers on the waiting list took up that option, although

The cowled instruments were simple and easy to read. These are seen on a right-hand-drive car.
MAGIC CAR PICS

THE Z3, 1995–1999

Having the hood up presented no major barriers to rearward visibility, thanks to the wide plastic window. Reversing could be tricky, though. MAGIC CAR PICS

THE 007 BOND EDITION

BMW followed up on the Z3's appearance in *GoldenEye* by offering US customers an 007 Bond Edition at Christmas 1995. The idea came from James McDowell, who was vice president of marketing at BMW North America, and it was executed in conjunction with mail-order company Neiman Marcus. The model was advertised in the Neiman Marcus Christmas catalogue with a price of $35,000 before delivery and taxes. In addition to the car, buyers would receive two tickets for a special *GoldenEye* dinner party to be held in Los Angeles, at which actor Pierce Brosnan (James Bond in the film) would be among the guests.

The original target was to sell 20 cars, but within two days of the catalogue's issue, orders for 100 cars had poured in. So BMW agreed to increase total production of the limited edition to 100 cars. These were built with identification numbers LE00700 to LE00799, and buyers were able to take delivery from spring 1996.

The cars were Z3 1.9 models, all painted in 'Bond Blue-Grey' (actually Atlanta Blue) like the car in the film, and had beige leather seats. Customers could choose between manual and automatic gearboxes. The cars had 7J x 16 split-spoke alloy wheels with 225/50 ZR 16 tyres, and the bodywork featured chrome accents (such as the door handles) and a chromed luggage rack on the boot lid. There was special roadster luggage, too.

The interior had wood trim on the dashboard centre stack, a wooden gear shift grip and a part-wood steering wheel. Other special features were a hi-fi system with a subwoofer and CD player, a cell phone mounted alongside the handbrake, special floor mats with an 007 motif, a wind deflector and a special commemorative plaque on the dashboard that read '007 James Bond Z3 roadster' but was not numbered.

---

it is not clear how many 318i convertibles BMW had to buy back. Those customers who had ordered a Z3 before June 1996 found their patience rewarded with a free RDS radio cassette unit on taking delivery.

There was certainly no shortage of customers for the Z3. More than 15,000 had been ordered globally by the time production began in autumn 1995 with left-hand-drive cars, and production of 318i models at Spartanburg was suspended in order to meet demand for the Z3. In July 1996, it was stopped altogether – which made great publicity copy for BMW but had probably been planned from the start.

The 4-cylinder Cars and the Press

The entry-level 1.8-litre car did not particularly impress those motoring journalists who tried one. Although its 121mph (194km/h) top speed was adequate, 10.5sec to reach 100km/h (62mph) from rest was nothing special. A 1.8-litre Mazda MX-5 might only reach 115mph (185km/h) but it was fractionally quicker to 100km/h and was a lot cheaper to buy.

In the UK, *Autosport* magazine tried a German-specification car for its issue dated 7 May 1996, and came away distinctly disappointed. If nothing else, this was confirmation that BMW had been right in not making the entry-level model available in the UK. *Autosport* found the car's handling to be fluid and entertaining, even in the wet, but the 'the old and less capable Mazda MX-5 proves more involving'. Performance was lacklustre, too: the 1.8-litre Z3 was

> *equipped with an image and profile that encourages [sic] expectations I fear are far beyond those that its pleasing but hardly-astonishing engines will be able to satisfy . . . it fails to realize its true potential by lacking the power to live up to the promise.*

The 1.9-litre car certainly brought worthwhile performance improvements. The five-speed car was a whole second faster than the 1.8-litre model to 100km/h (62mph) and had a higher maximum of 127mph too. Nevertheless, there were still some questions about its performance. Britain's *What Car?* magazine perceptively observed that roadster motoring was 'more about the joy of travelling than the speed, and the 1.9-litre engine should prove sufficiently brisk and relaxed for many owners'. The car was 'pleasing rather than thrilling to drive', but 'above all, you'll thoroughly enjoy driving and owning it'.

The one-marque magazine *BMW Car* tested one of the then-new right-hand-drive 1.9-litre Z3s for its April 1997 issue, concluding that 'BMW has succeeded in producing an appealing package at a reasonable price.' Minor niggles were poor three-quarter vision when the soft top was erected, and an inflexible tonneau cover that was very difficult to fit. The handling was 'a touch woolly for a sports car', and the performance was not startling. As Charles Armstrong-Wilson wrote:

> *Despite its 140bhp, it never feels like the gutsiest engine around but it will rev freely right up to the red*

Only the early 1.8-litre cars came with steel wheels. All other models had alloys of one sort or another.
MAGIC CAR PICS

THE Z3, 1995–1999

The wind deflector that fitted behind the seats of the Z3 really did reduce the buffeting that passengers in open cars experience at speed. BMW

line. In the Z3 it leaves the car feeling sluggish off the mark but, with a bit of momentum behind it and enthusiastic use of the gears, it can be rowed along quite rapidly and with great enjoyment.

BMW Car also took the sensible view of the 1.9-litre roadster's appeal:

Ultimates are often an acquired taste that can only be appreciated fully by an enlightened minority. The Z3's appeal is much broader. Drivers of varying skills can jump into the car and enjoy it instantly. It is reassuring and user friendly yet with enough spirit to make anyone want to have some fun with it. The chances are that if the car's detractors were offered the keys for a sunny weekend, few would be able to resist.

The Americans, too, were rather taken with the car. *Road & Track* complained in its January 1996 issue that the exhaust note was a little too refined for a roadster, but the magazine's Kim Reynolds did like the handling: 'Once you're accustomed to its roll angles, the Z3's handling balance and sheer flingability are positively acrobatic.' Even the ride quality was good, 'positively plush for a car that's still really small'. The Z3 was 'the best-riding, most structurally robust, open sports car in my memory'.

Performance testing revealed an astonishingly quick 8.1sec for the 0–60mph sprint, with an electronically governed 116mph (187km/h) top speed, but these features did not even rate a mention in the *Road & Track* narrative. Their absence spoke volumes about American expectations of an affordable roadster, and made it abundantly clear that BMW had got the recipe right for the Z3's most important market.

There was little doubt, however, that the 6-cylinder car would be the one to get enthusiast drivers really interested in the Z3. Or so it seemed in 1996.

THE Z3, 1995–1999

The 6-cylinder Model

Even though the Z3 design had been drawn up to accommodate BMW's small-block 6-cylinder engine, company spokesmen were rather evasive about what was planned when the 4-cylinder cars were introduced in 1995. They had clearly been told to say nothing about the forthcoming 6-cylinder in case it persuaded eager customers not to buy the 4-cylinder car but to wait for the introduction of the 6-cylinder model. The most they would admit was that a 6-cylinder model would go on sale if there was sufficient demand. But anyone who looked under the bonnet of a 4-cylinder Z3 could see that there was plenty of unused space ahead of the engine – enough, of course, for a longer 6-cylinder engine.

The 6-cylinder Z3 had been scheduled to enter production at Spartanburg in November 1995, just a couple of months after the two 4-cylinder models, but in practice it was delayed. One reason may have been last-minute changes to get the weight distribution right: the first 4-cylinder cars had their battery under the bonnet, but for the 6-cylinder this was moved to the boot, and the 4-cylinders followed suit when the 6-cylinder entered production. Meanwhile, BMW made the most of the publicity opportunities by previewing the car at the Geneva Motor Show in March 1996, although none would be available for sale before March 1997. A ride-and-drive event on Madeira introduced the Z3 2.8 to the motoring press earlier in the year, and the first road-test impressions were published in magazines dated March 1997. The availability of right-hand-drive cars lagged a little behind the rest, and those for the UK began to arrive in August 1997.

The key feature of the new Z3 2.8 was of course that 6-cylinder engine. Known as the M52 type, it was an all-alloy design that had made its debut in the 1995 E39 528i saloons and from 1996 had also been available in the E36 328i. From its 2793cc swept volume, it delivered 193bhp and a wide spread of torque thanks to BMW's technically advanced VANOS variable valve timing system. VANOS (VAriable NOckenwellen Steurung, or variable camshaft control) moved the inlet camshaft forwards or backwards in its housing hydraulically, so optimizing valve timing at all speeds to give maximum bottom-end torque as well as top-end power.

The 6-cylinder engine was some 41kg (90lb) heavier than the 4-cylinder types in the Z3, and this extra weight was

ASC + T TRACTION CONTROL

BMW's ASC + T (Automatic Stability Control and Traction) traction control system used the sensors of the ABS system to detect the wheelspin that accompanies a loss of traction, and automatically applied the brakes, reduced engine power, or both, in order to restore lost traction. It could be deactivated by a switch on the centre console.

the main reason why the battery was moved to the boot. Once it had been, the Z3 2.8 boasted an ideal weight distribution of 50 per cent over the front wheels and 50 per cent over the rear wheels. BMW's engineers had given the car stronger rear trailing arms, stiffer anti-roll bars, and recalibrated springs and dampers. There were also stronger wheel carriers incorporating larger bearings, and not surprisingly wider wheels and tyres as well. So the 16in alloys that were optional on the 4-cylinder cars became standard for the Z3 2.8, while a set of 17in wheels, wider at the rear than at the front, remained an extra-cost option.

The new engine delivered much more exciting performance than the 4-cylinder types. With the standard five-speed manual gearbox, a Z3 2.8 could reach 100km/h (62mph) from rest in 7.1sec, while the top speed was 135mph (217km/h). In the USA, where the car was electronically limited to 127mph – mainly to meet emissions targets – BMW claimed just 6.3sec for the 0–60mph sprint. Even US customers who chose the four-speed automatic option (which was not available in every market) were not short-changed, with a claimed 6.7sec 0–60mph time and the same 127mph electronically limited maximum. For reassurance, ASC + T traction control was standard equipment.

There were cosmetic differences from the 4-cylinder cars, too. Although there was still no badge on the tail to show that this was the 6-cylinder model, it was not hard for those in the know to recognize it. Most obvious were the twin exhausts that replaced the single tailpipe of the 4-cylinder cars, but running these a close second were wider rear wheel arches. At the front, a larger air intake in the apron was the key distinguishing feature. The cockpit

■ THE Z3, 1995–1999

There were no distinguishing badges on the tail of the 6-cylinder Z3 (see opposite) – but the fatter wheel arches were a ready recognition feature, as were the twin tailpipes. A comparison with the rear of a 4-cylinder car (see above) makes the differences clear.

THE WIESMANN HARDTOP

It is in the nature of the aftermarket parts industry that specialist companies eagerly examine any new 'enthusiast' car that reaches the market to find where they can offer add-ons not available from the manufacturer. The Z3 certainly fell into the category of an enthusiast car, and German custom hardtop specialist Wiesmann GmbH of Dülmen (in NordRhein-Westfalia) quickly identified the chance to design and market a demountable hardtop for it. It is likely that the Wiesmann hardtop reached the market before the factory-designed hardtop that became available in January 1998; it certainly remained available afterwards.

The Wiesmann hardtop was slightly more angular than the factory's own design, with a larger rear window. Two channels on the roof ducted rainwater towards the rear of the car, whereas the BMW hardtop had rubber strips that acted as guides. Like the BMW version, the Wiesmann hardtop required an installation kit to be mounted to the body of the car. Early kits were not suitable for cars with the later powered soft top, and Wiesmann later introduced a modified installation kit to suit these cars.

featured leather upholstery as standard, and for extra cost this could be had with a two-tone colour scheme. Burr walnut trim added a more upmarket feel, and there was the option of Chromeline trim, which featured chrome for the instrument bezels, headlight switch, handbrake release and interior door handles.

All these new features made the Z3 2.8 a much more expensive purchase than its 4-cylinder siblings. From BMW's point of view, it also gave them a model that could compete with prestigious rivals such as the latest Porsche Boxster and the Mercedes-Benz SLK. The strategy for the Z3 model range was gradually becoming clearer.

■ THE Z3, 1995–1999

BMW INDIVIDUAL AND THE Z3

BMW Individual had been established in 1991 as a bespoke finishing service that enabled customers to order a range of colours, interior trims and other cosmetic features that were not available on mainstream models. Customers could use it to create cars that were individual to their tastes and, perhaps more crucially, were likely to be different from any other BMW they would ever encounter. The service was not, however, available in the USA before 2006 because of regulations in that country that gave buyers the right to cancel specially ordered vehicles without penalty.

BMW Individual became available for the Z3 during 1997, with a range of small-volume special editions. There were different editions for different countries, but one interesting edition took the fight to the enemy in the home of Mazda. This Japanese special edition was based on the Z3 1.8 and had Sundown metallic paint (code 395) with an Extended Leather interior, which covered the dashboard and centre console in addition to the usual elements. The upholstery was in Cassis Nappa leather with black piping and the seats were heated. There was an M steering wheel coloured to match the upholstery, together with air conditioning, Chromeline interior highlights and velour floor mats. The optional M suspension was fitted, along with a 25 per cent limited-slip differential, and the turn-signal lenses were white instead of the standard amber.

When BMW Individual became available for the Z3 in 1997, there were several special 'launch editions'.

The 1998 Model Year

With the arrival of the Z3 2.8, BMW's plan for expanding the Z3 range was getting into its stride. The new model had barely been announced when BMW followed up with a second 6-cylinder type, this time developed by its M division and bearing the title of M Roadster. Although deliveries of this car began in Europe in the late spring of 1997, there would be a special version of it for the USA and this would not go on sale until early 1998. The full story of the high-performance M derivatives of the Z3 range is told in Chapter 5.

Developments seemed to follow thick and fast during 1997. Shortly after the Z3 2.8 cars went on sale, a scoop photographer caught a coupé variant of the Z3 on test at the Nürburgring. Then late October 1997 brought ample illustration of the Z3's success when the 100,000th example was built at Spartanburg – less than two years after production had begun. New for the 1998 model year was power operation for the roadster's convertible roof. This became an extra-cost option on the 4-cylinder cars but was made standard on the 6-cylinder models in some countries, including the UK and the USA.

THE 100,000TH Z3

The 100,000th Z3 was a silver 2.8-litre model built to the personal specification of Richard Medcalf, a butcher and farmer from Yorkshire, England, who had ordered a 6-cylinder Z3 as a wedding present for his fiancée, Celia Knight.

When it became clear that Richard's car would become the 100,000th Z3, BMW arranged a special ceremony. He and Celia were flown to the Spartanburg factory as guests of BMW Manufacturing Corporation USA to watch it come off the assembly line. The couple also took part in BMW's commemorative open day celebrations on 1 November, where they met the Governor of South Carolina, David Beasley, and were formally presented with their car.

The 100,000th Z3 leaves the assembly line at Spartanburg in October 1997. It would be delivered to a British couple who were invited over for the occasion.

■ THE Z3, 1995–1999

BMW's own optional hardtop was characterized by black rubber rain guides on the roof. WIKIMEDIA/BEEMWEJ

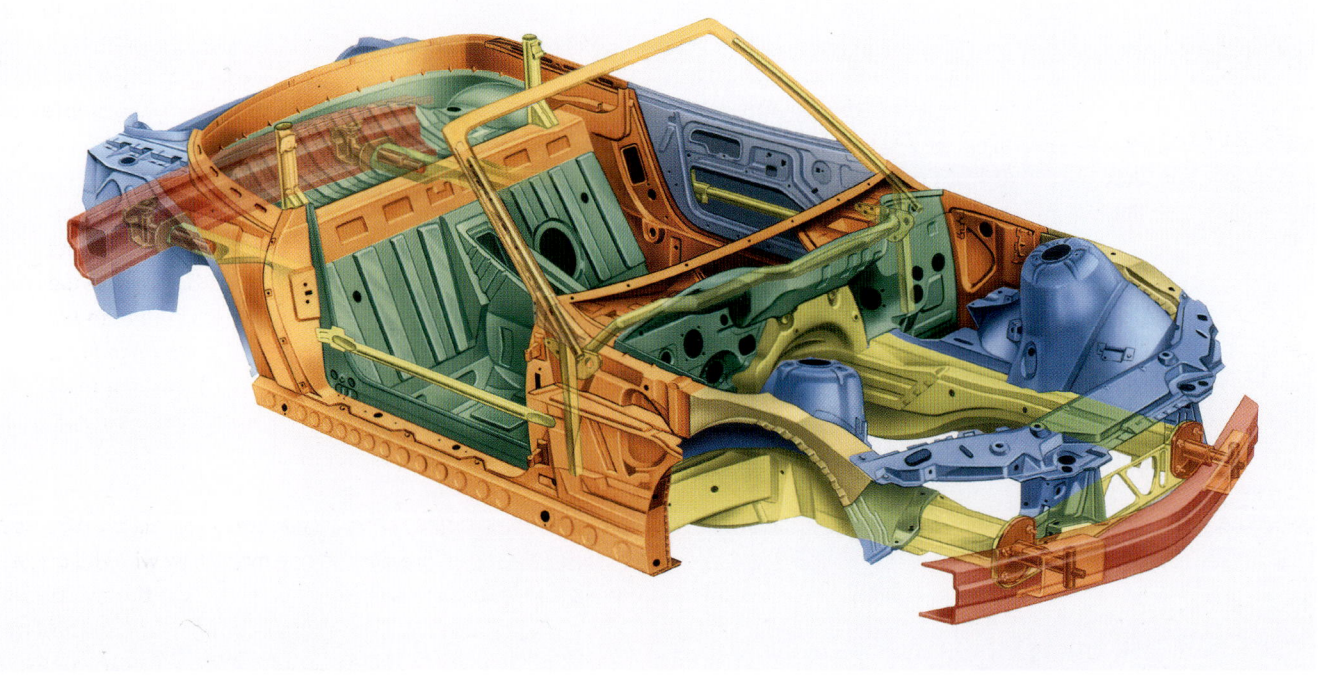

A variety of different steel types created the strong bodyshell of the Z3. It was very rigid indeed for an open two-seater – although critics sometimes complained that a stiffer shell would have given better handling.

The major components were packed tightly into the space available, as this cutaway drawing of an early Z3 shows.

Several other new features were added for the 1998 model year. Most obvious was a pair of rollover protection bars behind the seats – BMW's response to the ingenious pop-up rollover bars in the rival Mercedes-Benz SLK models. A power-operated roof was a further welcome addition to the specification. All Z3s now came with pre-wiring for a CD changer, which became a separate extra-cost option. At the same time, ASC + T traction control became standard on the 1.9-litre models, as did a driver's side vanity mirror and a storage net in the passenger footwell.

Yet another new option was introduced in January 1998. This was a demountable hardtop, quite possibly prompted by news of the hardtop that Porsche produced for its Boxster: BMW could not afford to be left behind. The Z3 hardtop was made of aluminium alloy, came with a heated rear window, and a BMW dealer had to mount a special installation kit to the car before it could be fitted. It was expensive from the start, but Z3 owners adopted it enthusiastically.

The Z3 2.8 and the Press

Motoring writers everywhere welcomed the Z3 2.8 with open arms. In Britain, *Motor Sport* magazine published impressions in its February 1997 issue, summarising the model very neatly: 'If what you're after is a roadster with traditional values applied in a thoroughly modern but respectful manner, it gets close to the bullseye.' There was only one real drawback: the car had 'a chassis of consummate ability which needs a little more character to really sparkle'.

Specialist *BMW Car* magazine was also deeply impressed. In its September 1997 issue, its report read:

> *Gun the engine through the gears and the 2.8 scorches off the line with the sort of energy alien to its 4-cylinder brother. If you have just 1,500rpm on the clock in the lower gears, every caress of the throttle produces an instant response . . . the low-end grunt is now sufficient for the driver to influence the car's cornering attitude on throttle and steering. Purists will agree that this is a prerequisite for a real driver's car.*

In the USA, *Automobile Magazine* stated in its March 1997 issue that 'the Z3 2.8 addresses the one major flaw with the original: a nice car looking for a real engine. . . . It's now the sports car it always promised to be.' That same month, *Motor Trend* echoed these sentiments, enthusing that the 6-cylinder car 'combines all the inherent goodness of a standard Z3 with a bonus pack of extra abilities you didn't know were missing'. It seemed that BMW had definitely got the formula right this time.

THE Z3, 1995–1999

The Coupé

There was an interesting story behind the coupé derivative of the Z3 that had been caught on test in spring 1997. No such model had been envisaged in the original plans for the range, but once a full-size mock-up had been built it became obvious to some of the engineers involved with the project that a coupé derivative would be feasible.

The story goes that five of them decided to design such a car as a private venture in their own time, and that they commandeered a car (presumably a prototype) and modified it in the underground car park at BMW Technik. The coupé roof was supposedly constructed using old-fashioned 'knife and fork' methods, and no computer-aided design was involved. At one stage, the rear side windows had the characteristic BMW hockey-stick shape to their trailing edges, but in the end opinions gelled around a straight edge. A friendly member of the styling team certainly lent a hand to advise on matters of detail at a late stage in the project. BMW's research chief Wolfgang Reitzle was then shown the completed vehicle.

A key advantage of the coupé design was that the fixed roof would make the Z3's body more rigid, both structurally and torsionally. A key disadvantage was that it was not very attractive, and the mock-up seems to have polarized opinions within BMW. Nevertheless, costings proved that it could be done profitably as long as the basic body shape and panels of the roadster were retained, and so a coupé entered the range in autumn 1998 as a 1999 model. Within BMW, it was known as the E36/8 type.

The coupé body was only ever made available with the 6-cylinder engine options, and in some countries not all of those were made available. In the UK, for example, it was available only as an M Coupé (see Chapter 4) and the 2.8-litre engine that was offered elsewhere did not become available. The promised additional body rigidity was matched by an element of practicality, for the coupé had more space behind the seats than was available in the roadster's boot – 210ltr (7.4cu ft) of it as against 165ltr (5.8cu ft) in the open car. This was reached through a top-hinged hatchback that carried a small spoiler just above the rear window. Extra-cost options were a storage net for the load space and a sunroof.

Most interesting, perhaps, was that the rear end of the coupé sported notched light units. It seemed like a practical expedient to allow the lights to wrap around the lower corners of the hatch, but what observers did not know at the time was that notched light units were planned for introduction across the Z3 model range (M models excepted) for the 2000 model year.

The Z3 Coupé was not everybody's idea of a resolved design, and soon acquired the nickname of the 'breadvan'. Available only with the 6-cylinder engines – this is a 2.8-litre car – it nevertheless added an interesting dimension to the range.

THE Z3, 1995–1999

The 1999 Model Year

The planned facelift for the Z3 was still in the future as the 1999 model year opened in autumn 1998, but there was plenty of excitement in the new line-up. No fewer than three new engines became available for the mainstream cars; the coupé went on sale; and there were some other novelties as well. Meanwhile, the slow-selling automatic gearbox option for the 4-cylinder models was quietly dropped from the catalogues.

At the bottom of the range, the 1.8-litre engine was replaced by a detuned version of the M44 engine in the 1.9-litre models. With 118bhp at 5,500rpm and 133lb ft at 3,900rpm it was a little more powerful and torquey than the outgoing type, but the performance differential between the Z3 1.8 and the Z3 1.9 was maintained. The main benefit of the change to BMW was that it simplified parts logistics: there was now one basic 4-cylinder engine in the Z3 instead of two different ones.

For the US market, the change made no difference as the Z3 1.8 model was not available there. However, there was a related change: the Z3 1.9 was withdrawn from the line-up (although it remained available in other countries, such as the UK) and was replaced by a new 6-cylinder car.

> **THE SPECIAL EDITIONS, 1999**
>
> Two special editions of the Z3 were introduced on 1 April 1999 to help generate showroom traffic and clear old stocks before the arrival of the 2000 model year cars. These were called the Fiji and the Orinoco. Both drew on the range of special options available through the BMW Individual personalization service.
>
> The Fiji was available with either the 1.9-litre or the 2.8-litre engine. It came with Fiji Green (code 413) paint and with a two-tone dark blue and black interior featuring green piping. The soft top was black and the car had white turn-signal lenses in place of the standard amber type.
>
> The Orinoco was also available with either the 1.9-litre or the 2.8-litre engine. It came with Orinoco metallic (406) paint and cream seats with contrasting piping. The soft top was beige or black and the car had white turn-signal lenses in place of the standard amber type.

The convertible top folded away neatly behind the seats and, on later cars like this one, two sturdy rollover hoops protected the car's occupants against the worst eventuality. With optional contrasting colours, as seen on this UK-market car, the interior could be made most attractive.

THE Z3, 1995–1999

Z3 PAINT OPTIONS, 1996–99 MODELS

1996 model year

Colour/BMW code	Colour/BMW code
Arctic Silver metallic 309	Jet Black 668
Atlanta Blue metallic 306	Montreal Blue metallic 297
Bright Red 314	Turquoise Green 326
Cayenne Red metallic 520	Violet Red 328
Dark Green metallic 307	

1997 model year

Colour/BMW code	Colour/BMW code
Alpine White 300	Dark Green metallic 307
Arctic Silver metallic 309	Jet Black 668
Atlanta Blue metallic 306	Montreal Blue metallic 297
Boston Green metallic 275	Turquoise Green 326
Bright Red 314	Violet Red 328

Dark Green, Turquoise Green and Violet Red were listed as Special Order colours and cost extra.

1998 model year

Colour/BMW code	Colour/BMW code
Alpine White 300	Dark Green metallic 307
Arctic Silver metallic 309	Jet Black 668
Atlanta Blue metallic 306	Montreal Blue metallic 297
Boston Green metallic 275	Turquoise Green 326
Bright Red 314	Violet Red328
Dakar Yellow 337	

1999 model year

Colour/BMW code	Colour/BMW code
Alpine White 300	Jet Black 668
Arctic Silver metallic 309	Montreal Blue metallic 297
Atlanta Blue metallic 306	Steel Gray metallic 400
Boston Green metallic 275	Turquoise Green metallic 326
Bright Red 314	Violet Red 328
Dark Green metallic 307	

This meant that the US model line-up for the Z3 range now consisted of only 6-cylinder types.

The new entry-level model for North America was not made available in other countries, except for some of those that took North American-specification cars as a matter of course. It came only as a roadster, and was carefully priced not to discourage buyers at the lower end of the Z3 range. In fact, its base price of $30,520 was just $1,500 (less than 5 per cent) more than the 4-cylinder Z3 1.9 had cost in 1997, which made the car something of a bargain. The new Z3 2.3 came with the five-speed manual gearbox as standard and the four-speed automatic as an extra-cost option, and except for its engine was in all respects similar to the Z3 2.8. It had that car's wider rear wings, stronger rear trailing arms, stiffer anti-roll bars and heftier wheel carriers with larger bearings.

The designation of Z3 2.3 was not entirely accurate, but had almost certainly been chosen to show that the model was a direct competitor for the Mercedes-Benz SLK 230. In fact, the engine in the new BMW model had a swept volume of nearly 2.5 litres. It was the 170bhp 2494cc version of the M52 6-cylinder, as used in the equally oddly named 323i models that had been introduced in 1996. It featured the latest Double-VANOS system, in which both inlet and exhaust camshafts could be adjusted automatically to suit the valve timing to the demands on the engine. With the refinement of the 6-cylinder engine came the same electronically limited 127mph top speed as in the Z3 2.8 but less acceleration. BMW claimed 7.3sec for the 0–60mph sprint with a manual gearbox and 7.7sec with the automatic option. Both were big improvements over the old Z3 1.9.

The third new engine for 1999 was really an old one in a new guise. It was the 2.8-litre M52 6-cylinder upgraded with the same Double-VANOS system as in the 2.3-litre engine. All Z3 2.8 models received it at the same time, and the new engine brought improvements in emissions and drivability, although it was actually rated at the same 190bhp (or 189bhp in North America) as before.

The New Z3s and the Press

In Britain, *BMW Car* magazine tried a 1.8-litre car with the new engine for its May 2000 issue. It concluded that 'the 1.8 may be no muscle car, but it delivers a fairly solid push at low revs. Just enough to make it feel lively in the urban flow, not what we expected at all.' Even so, the car needed 10.2sec to reach 100km/h (62mph) from rest, which made it around 2sec slower than either of its obvious rivals, the Mazda MX-5 and MGF.

Meanwhile, the North American Z3 2.3 was even better than BMW's performance claims suggested. *Road & Track* magazine's Douglas Kott managed a 0–60mph time of just 6.7sec, which was barely short of what a Z3 2.8 could achieve. As that magazine noted in its July 1998 appraisal, the new model 'forever dispels the notion that the base-model Z3 is simply a [Mazda] Miata clone with a $10,000 price premium justified by the spinning-propellor badge on its clamshell hood'.

Z3 SPECIFICATIONS, 1996–99 MODELS

Engines
1.8-litre (1996–98)
Type M43B18 4-cylinder petrol
1796cc (84 × 81mm)
Single ohc, chain-driven
2v per cylinder
Five-bearing crankshaft
Compression ratio 10.0:1
Bosch Motronic M1.7 engine management system
Three-way catalytic converter standard
116PS (114bhp) at 5,500rpm
168Nm (124lb ft) at 3,000rpm

1.8-litre (1999)
Type M43B18 4-cylinder petrol
1895cc (83.5 × 85mm)
Single ohc, chain-driven
2v per cylinder
Five-bearing crankshaft
Compression ratio 9.7:1
BMS46 engine management system
Three-way catalytic converter standard
120PS (118bhp) at 5,500rpm
180Nm (133lb ft) at 3,900rpm

1.9-litre
Type M44B19 4-cylinder petrol
1895cc (85 × 83.5mm)
Twin ohc, chain-driven
4v per cylinder
Five-bearing crankshaft
Compression ratio 10.0:1
DME 5.2 engine management system, sequential port injection
Three-way catalytic converter standard
140PS (138bhp) at 6,000rpm
180Nm (133lb ft) at 4,300rpm

2.3-litre
Type M52B23 6-cylinder petrol
2494cc (84 × 75mm)
Twin ohc, chain-driven
4v per cylinder
Double-VANOS variable valve timing
Seven-bearing crankshaft
Compression ratio 10.5:1
Bosch Motronic engine management system giving sequential port injection
Three-way catalytic converter standard
172PS (170bhp) at 5,500rpm
246Nm (181lb ft) at 3,500rpm

2.8-litre (Single-VANOS, 1997–98)
Type M52B28 6-cylinder petrol
2793cc (84 × 84mm)
Twin ohc, chain-driven
4v per cylinder
VANOS variable valve timing
Seven-bearing crankshaft
Compression ratio 10.2:1
Bosch Motronic engine management system giving sequential port injection
Three-way catalytic converter standard
European engines:
193PS (190bhp) at 5,500rpm
278Nm (206lb ft) at 3,500rpm
North American engines:
189bhp at 5,300rpm
203lb ft at 3,950rpm

2.8-litre (Double-VANOS, 1999)
Type M52B28 6-cylinder petrol
2793cc (84 × 84mm)

(continued overleaf...)

(continued from previous page)

Twin ohc, chain-driven
4v per cylinder
Double-VANOS variable valve timing
Seven-bearing crankshaft
Compression ratio 10.2:1
Siemens engine management system
Three-way catalytic converter standard
European engines:
193PS (190bhp) at 5,500rpm
278Nm (206lb ft) at 3,500rpm
North American engines:
189bhp at 5,300rpm
203lb ft at 3,950rpm

Transmission
Five-speed manual gearbox standard
    Ratios 4.23:1, 2.53:1, 1.66:1, 1.22:1, 1.00:1 (1.8, 1.9, 2.0 and 2.2i)
    Ratios 4.20:1, 2.49:1, 1.66:1, 1.24:1, 1.00:1 (2.3, 2.8, 3.0i)
Four-speed ZF automatic gearbox optional, 1995–98; also on 2.0, 1999–2000
    Ratios 2.40:1, 1.47:1, 1.00:1, 0.72:1
Five-speed ZF automatic gearbox with AGS optional, 2000–2002
    Ratios 3.42:1, 2.52:1, 1.61:1, 1.00:1, 0.75:1 (2.2i, 3.0i)

Axle ratio
3.07:1   (3.0i manual)
3.15:1   (2.3 and 2.8 manual, 3.0i automatic))
3.38:1   (2.2i manual)
3.45:1   (1.8, 1.9 and 2.0 manual; 2.2i auto)
3.23:1   with S52 engine
3.15:1   with S50 and S54 engines

Suspension, steering and brakes
Front suspension with MacPherson struts, lower L-arms and anti-roll bar
Rear suspension with semi-trailing arms, separate springs and dampers, and anti-roll bar
Rack-and-pinion steering with 16.8:1 ratio (1.8 models) or 13.9:1 ratio (1.9, 2.3 and 2.8 models) and standard power assistance
Disc brakes all round, with twin hydraulic circuits; ABS optional on Z3 1.8 to 1998 and standard on other models
Z3 1.8 286mm (11.26in) front discs
    228.6mm (9in) rear discs
Z3 1.9 286mm (11.26in) front discs
    280mm (11in) rear discs
Z3 2.3 286mm (11.26in) ventilated front discs
    280mm (11in) solid rear discs
Z3 2.8 (to 1998) 286mm (11.26in) front discs
    280mm (11in) rear discs
Z3 2.8 (1999) 286mm (11.26in) ventilated front discs
    280mm (11in) solid rear discs

Dimensions

Overall length	4,025mm (158.5in)
Overall width	1,692mm (66.6in)
Overall height	1,288mm (50.7in)
Wheelbase	2,446mm (96.3in)
Front track	1411/1423mm (55.5/56.0in), dependent on tyre size
Rear track	1427/1439mm (56.2/56/6in), dependent on tyre size

Wheels and tyres
6.5J x 15 steel wheels with 205/60 HR 15 tyres Z3 1.8 only
7J x 16 five-spoke alloy wheels, with 225/50 ZR 16 tyres standard on Z3 1.9 for USA, on Z3 2.3 and Z3 2.8; optional on Z3 1.8
7.5J x 17 five-spoke alloy wheels, with 225/45 ZR 17 tyres optional on all models
7.5J x 17 front and 8.5J x 17 rear alloy wheels with 225/50 ZR 17 and 245/40 ZR 17 tyres optional on Z3 1.9, Z3 2.3 and Z3 2.8

Unladen weights

1.8 Roadster	1,160kg (2,557lb)
1.9 Roadster	1,185kg (2,612lb)
2.3 Roadster	1,315kg (2,899lb) with manual gearbox
	1,355kg (2,987lb) with automatic gearbox
2.8 Roadster	1,260kg (2,778lb)
2.8 Roadster (US)	1,320kg (2,910lb) with manual gearbox
	1,360kg (2,998lb) with automatic gearbox
2.8 Coupé	1,300kg (2,866lb)

THE Z3, 1995–1999

The Z3 was certainly compact, but also roomy enough to make a comfortable two-seat roadster. These were the main dimensions.

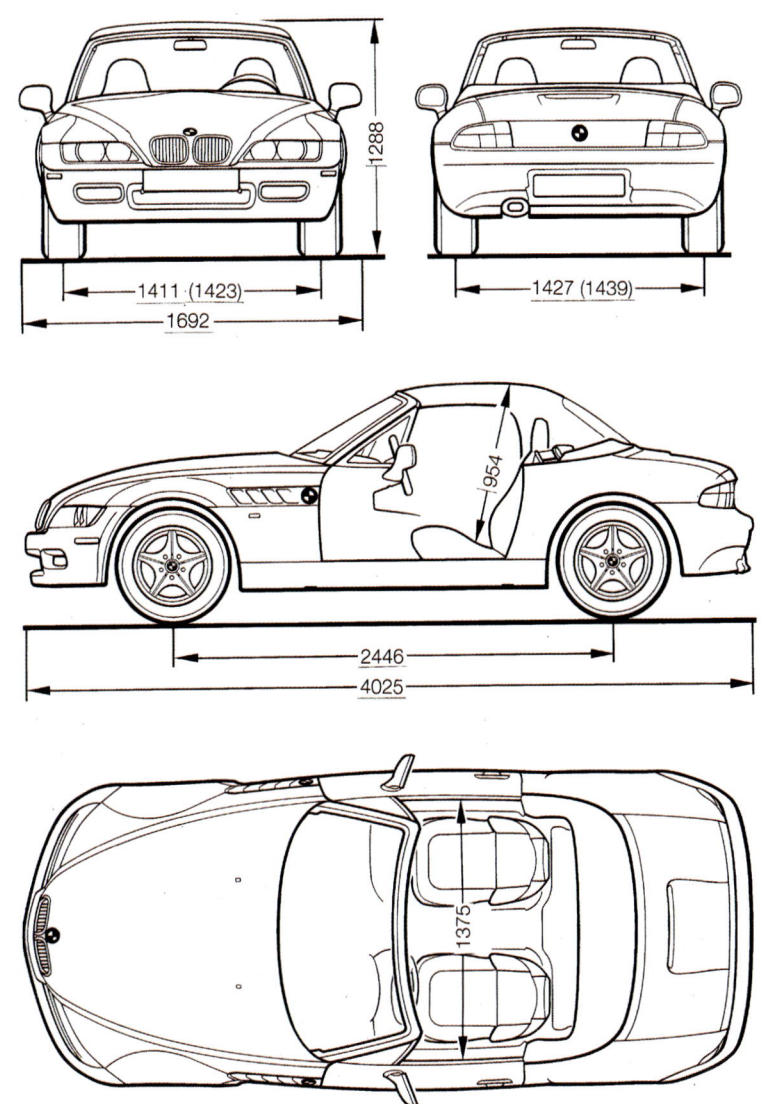

Z3 PERFORMANCE FIGURES, 1996–99 MODELS

1.8 Roadster	0–60mph	10.1sec
	Maximum	121mph (194km/h)
1.9 Roadster	0–60mph	9.1sec
	Maximum	127mph (205km/h)
2.8 Roadster	0–60mph	6.6sec
	Maximum	144mph (231km/h)
2.8 Coupé	0–60mph	6.5sec
	Maximum	144mph (231km/h)

CHAPTER THREE

THE Z3, 2000–2002

BMW had maintained the momentum of the Z3 range very effectively in its first four years of production, introducing new models and altering specifications with laudable frequency. Nevertheless, the changes it made for the 2000 model year were the most far-reaching yet. The company was well practised at judging when its ranges needed to be refreshed to keep them from becoming stale, and the 2000 models brought changes in three areas. First and most obvious was a facelift. Second was a set of interior changes, and third was yet more new engines.

The Facelifted 2000 Models

Production of the facelifted cars actually began in April 1999. This time, the bodyshell design was rationalized and both 4-cylinder and 6-cylinder cars shared a common shell. The most obvious changes were at the tail of the roadsters, where the rear wheel arches were higher and wider than before, with a more exaggerated curve that matched the shape of the front arches better.

At the same time, roadsters gained a new boot-lid panel, its top surface slightly higher than before to match the new wing line and its lower edges notched to accommodate new tail-light units with the L-shape characteristic of other contemporary BMWs. These lights were nevertheless not the same as the notched units on the coupés. The 2.8-litre cars took on a clear lens for the third brake light mounted on the boot lid, although other models still had a red lens, and they also gained chromed exhaust tips. The release button for the boot lid took on a chrome surround, and model badges appeared for the first time next to it.

This UK-market Z3 2.0 shows off the new rear end, with restyled wings and L-shaped lamp units. Also in evidence is one of the attractive new alloy wheel styles.

THE Z3, 2000–2002

Early Z3s were known by their engine size; the later ones took on an 'i' after the designation, as seen here.
MAGIC CAR PICS

The new L-shaped tail-light clusters added some interest to the rear of the car. This one is seen on an early 2.0 model.

At the front of the cars, chrome bezels around the headlamps provided greater definition. The twin grilles were also slightly reshaped and all models now took on the 6-cylinder style of front apron with its more pronounced lower lip. On US models, the 2.8-litre cars gained fog lights as standard, although these remained optional on other variants. Overall, the result of the exterior changes was a slightly more aggressive and sporty appearance, and a definite improvement over the almost tentative shape of the earlier cars. New paint colours of course accompanied the facelift, six for the US market but only five for the UK, and both the 16in and 17in wheel options now came with new designs.

Probably the most obvious change to the interior was that the soft top finally gained a headlining – a major omission from the earlier Z3s that had occasioned a good deal of adverse comment. There were now three layers of insulation rather than just one. The centre console also changed, taking on the switchgear from the M Roadster with repositioned controls and a new analogue clock in the middle. All cars had a new and sportier three-spoke steering wheel, and the standard audio system now came with larger and more powerful speakers. Chrome highlights and wood trim were still available as extra-cost upgrades, and there were three new colours available for the four choices of upholstery. A further option was side airbags, which came with redesigned door trims incorporating separate airbag cover panels.

As for the engines, BMW continued its policy of moving the Z3 upmarket and away from cars like the Mazda MX-5

■ THE Z3, 2000–2002

Even though the coupé models had pioneered L-shaped tail lamps in the Z3 range, this assembly-line picture shows quite clearly that they were not the same as those introduced on roadsters for the 2000 model year.

and the MGF by adding another 6-cylinder type to the range. The 1999 mainstream Z3 range had included the Z3 2.3 (with 2.5-litre engine) for North America and the Z3 2.8 for global markets, and now the 1991cc variant of the Double-VANOS M52 engine became available in a new model called the Z3 2.0.

This 150bhp engine was not made available for North America, but in other markets it replaced the Z3 1.9 4-cylinder model. In Europe it was expected to become the core model of the range and to account for the lion's share of sales. Delivering 0–100km/h (62mph) acceleration of 8.9sec with a manual gearbox, and going on to a maximum of 130mph (209km/h), it was a much more tempting proposition than the 4-cylinder car had been, bringing with it 6-cylinder refinement as well as that extra performance.

Three more changes for the 2000 model year need to

THE Z3, 2000–2002

ABOVE: All the facelifted Z3s for 2000 had the deeper 6-cylinder style of front spoiler, and all had chrome bezels around the headlamps behind their aerodynamic glass covers. This is actually a Z3 2.0 model.

RIGHT: Yet another style of alloy wheel, this time seen on the 2.8-litre car.

be recorded. First, BMW introduced an optional Speedster Cover, which provided streamlined fairings behind the seats. This was an accessory that did not prove popular. Much more useful was the arrival of wider rear tracks on all models, which aided handling stability. The third was a switch from the ASC + T traction control system to a new and more comprehensive system that BMW called DSC.

Those letters stood for Dynamic Stability Control. Like the earlier system, DSC could detect and compensate for a loss of traction. However, it could also compensate for oversteer and understeer by operating individual wheel brakes through the ABS system. Additional sensors provided information about the car's speed, steering angle, cornering force, brake pressure and the car's rotation around

■ THE Z3, 2000–2002

The Z3's boot was never very large, and looked even smaller when the hood bag was stowed in it.

All that extra space at the front of the engine bay made much better sense when the 6-cylinder model was introduced in 1997 after a 1996 preview. The engine was BMW's 2.8-litre M52, at this stage with single VANOS.

THE Z3, 2000–2002

There was nothing spectacular about the rotary controls for the heating and ventilating system, but they were clear and easy to use.
MAGIC CAR PICS

The optional Speedster Cover divided opinions. Some thought it added a neat touch of streamlining and style, but others thought it did not fit as snugly as a genuine BMW accessory should. Although it was introduced during 2000, this factory picture shows it on an earlier car.

55

■ THE Z3, 2000–2002

its vertical axis, and the processor was fully integrated with the engine management system. Like the earlier ASC + T system, DSC could be deactivated by a button on the centre console and, as before, it was an extra-cost option.

What the Press Thought

'Our choice would be one of the 6-cylinder cars,' wrote *BMW Car*'s Bob Harper after testing all the 2000 model year Z3s for the magazine's August 1999 issue.

The 2.0-litre car in particular represents excellent value for money. It is moderately quick . . . and handles well despite some initial understeer. Most importantly, the free-revving engine sounds wonderful, and it is fun to flick up and down the gearbox.

Harper considered the car a better bet than the more expensive Z3 2.8, and suggested that the cost savings made on buying the smaller-engined model could sensibly be invested in wider wheels, the DSC traction control option and leather upholstery.

However, this car did not address all the shortcomings of the earlier Z3 roadsters.

There are some niggles that really should have been addressed by the restyle. The tonneau cover is a truly dreadful design: if you value your fingernails you would do better to look at a rival's products. The Z3 is also not a pleasant environment for those over about 5ft 10in, as you sit too high in the car with your forehead exposed to the full force of the wind with the hood down, and you head will be touching the hood lining when it is up.

Worse was to come when the magazine tested a Z3 2.0 back-to-back with an example of the Z3 1.9 which it had replaced. The older 4-cylinder car showed itself to have more character than the new 6-cylinder, despite the latter's better performance and refinement. 'Ultimately,' argued Charles Armstrong-Wilson in the January 2000 issue, 'what matters is not how fast you are travelling, but how fast it feels. Judging by this parameter, the new car is slower than the old.'

Autocar also reported on the new model during 1999, noting that fuel economy had suffered even though performance had improved. As Peter Robinson wrote:

A most enjoyable car: this 2000-model Z3 2.8 belonged to BMW GB's press fleet, and is seen here during a long motorway run on a sunny weekend – with the top down, of course.

Down the road, the six is certainly more refined, yet the Z3's dearth of inspiration remains when you're playing sports car driver. The engine feels surprisingly inert and the whole experience is, well, unsporting... like many small sixes, the BMW lacks low-end torque ... the engine isn't especially responsive and needs to be revved above 4,000rpm to deliver any meaningful performance.

Despite the latest improvements, the Z3 2.0 was therefore still a flawed car. In the face of competition from the second-generation Mazda MX-5 (introduced in 1998), the Lotus Elise and the Alfa Romeo Spider, the sales battle looked as if it would become much tougher for BMW's two-seater.

The Individual Editions

Ever since 1997, a small number of cars had been personalized under the BMW Individual scheme. However, during the 2000 model year the company saw an opportunity to publicize the scheme further and also to increase sales of the Z3 2.0 models in advance of their planned demise. For although the Z3 2.0 was a new model for the 2000 model year, it had always been planned as a short-term expedient; another new engine was planned for 2001.

So it was that no fewer than four special editions of the Z3 roadster were introduced in February 2000, roughly midway through the model year. It is not clear which countries took them, but they were certainly available in the UK where each one cost the same £26,900 without extras. All seem to have had manual gearboxes, and the key features that distinguished them were their paint and trim.

The four special editions were all named after their special paint colours. These were Aegean Blue (code 336), Cosmos Black (code 303), Mora Red (code 359) and Velvet Blue (code 379). All appear to have had cream leather upholstery, and all had 7J x 16 alloy wheels.

The 2001 Model Year

The M52 6-cylinder engines, so recently upgraded to feature Double-VANOS, were due to go out of production during 2000. The primary reason was the impending arrival of new emissions regulations, the EU3/D4 regulations in Europe and the ULEV (Ultra Low Emissions Vehicle) regulations in the USA. BMW had decided to meet these by redesigning

From mid-2000, the new top model was the Z3 3.0i. This car is shown with its top down but side windows up – just as so many owners drove their Z3s. MAGIC CAR PICS

THE Z3, 2000–2002

This overhead view of the 3.0i makes clear how snug the car really was, despite the optical illusion of size fostered by its long bonnet. MAGIC CAR PICS

the combustion chamber of the 6-cylinder engines, and the associated changes made the engines different enough to merit the new designation of M54.

All this led to yet another shuffle of engines within the Z3 range, which during the 2000 model year had used M52 engines in the Z3 2.0, Z3 2.3 and Z3 2.8 models. (There was also the M division's S52 derivative in the M models, which are discussed in Chapter 4.) For 2001, the new Z3 2.2i replaced the European Z3 2.0, a Z3 2.5i replaced the North American Z3 2.3, and a Z3 3.0i replaced the Z3 2.8 for all markets: the use of the 'i' in the model names was a departure for the Z3. Availability of the new models began in July 2000.

The change brought three new engines, all of the M54 family. They had swept volumes of 2171cc (in the 2.2i), 2494cc (in the 2,5i) and 2979cc (in the 3.0i). These were all-alloy types with a four-valve configuration and Double-VANOS variable valve timing. Compared with the M52s they replaced, they had better combustion efficiency with a redesigned gas flow system that gave better fuel-air mixing, and smoother and cleaner performance at low speeds. They revved more freely than their M52 predecessors, and both had a slightly higher redline. Major benefits included better mid-range torque, with 85 per cent of the maximum available all the way from 1,500rpm to 6,000rpm. Both engines also used the electronic 'drive-by-wire' accelerator that had

THE Z3, 2000–2002

This was the new era: all model designations were now followed by an 'i' – which had originally stood for 'injection' and had been intended to distinguish petrol-powered BMWs from diesels with similar-sized engines. MAGIC CAR PICS

The 3.0i had yet another attractive design of multi-spoke alloy wheels. MAGIC CAR PICS

been pioneered on the BMW V12 engines and could provide smoother takeup of power. On top of that, there were improved catalytic converters to assist in reducing harmful exhaust emissions.

So the 2001 model year Z3 was now available with four mainstream engine options – plus, of course, the special M division engine in the M Roadster and M Coupé models which, as Chapter 4 explains, also went over to a derivative of the new M54 6-cylinder for 2001. Those four went into the Z3 1.9i (available only as a roadster and with a European specification), the Z3 2.2i (again roadster only, for Europe), the Z3 2.5i (roadster only, for the USA) and the Z3 3.0i (available as roadster or coupé, with both European and US specifications).

The new 2.2i model boasted 170bhp and was much more powerful and flexible than the older 2.0-litre. The 2.5i had 184bhp, and the new 3.0i with 231bhp completely outperformed the old Z3 2.8. With a manual gearbox, it despatched the 0–100km/h (0–62mph) sprint in 6.0sec, which was getting close to M division territory, and its 149mph (240km/h) top speed did not leave much of an advantage to the M Roadster and M Coupé with their electronically governed 155mph maximum.

With these new models came new automatic gearboxes, now with five speeds rather than the earlier four, although five-speed manual gearboxes remained standard equipment. The new automatics came as standard with BMW's Adaptive Gearbox System (AGS), which had been available elsewhere in range since 1995. AGS automatically adjusted the

■ THE Z3, 2000–2002

Seen directly from the side, the proportions of the Z3 coupé aroused controversy, but the rear three-quarters view was much less contentious. This is a 3.0i model.

The 3.0i had the latest M54 6-cylinder engine – although its main distinguishing characteristic in this underbonnet view is the style of plastic cover used! MAGIC CAR PICS

The two-tone leather upholstery in this 3.0i works on two levels: the colour combination of black and blue is subtle, and yet the shapes of the panels are eye-catching. MAGIC CAR PICS

change-up points in the gearbox to suit the driver's style. Its electronic control system was preprogrammed with two Economy programmes for everyday driving, two Sports programmes for fast driving, and a fifth programme that 'learned' any style not catered for by the other four. The whole system was completely automatic and changed seamlessly between programmes to suit the driver's mood or to suit the styles of different drivers.

From February 2001, midway through the 2001 model year, BMW made all four mainstream Z3 models – 1.9i, 2.2i, 2.5i and 3.0i – available in Sport Edition form. Despite the name, this was not actually a special edition but rather an option package that, in the USA, cost $3,000. On the outside, it consisted of a slightly different front bumper and 17in multi-spoke wheels on mildly lowered suspension. The inside came with brushed aluminium trim, an M steering wheel with tricolour stitching and an illuminated M gear lever. The seats were sports types, usually with two-tone upholstery and interior trim to match.

At the same time, European markets were offered a pair of special-edition models with the 2.2-litre engine. Both had 17in wheels, the Sapphire Edition coming with Black Sapphire (code 375) paint and the Titanium Edition being painted in Titanium silver metallic (code 354). Both cost the same £25,950 in the UK.

This is the centre console of the 3.0i, with Steptronic automatic gearbox. Note the digital clock below the heater controls, fitting into the position earlier occupied by an analogue clock. MAGIC CAR PICS

■ THE Z3, 2000–2002

ABOVE AND BELOW: The 2001 Sport Edition was really an option package, and is seen here on a 2.2i model. The attractive wheels had a 17in size.

THE Z3, 2000–2002

What the Press Thought

BMW Car compared a Z3 2.2i against a Fiat Barchetta roadster for its May 2001 issue, concluding that 'ultimately the Z3 doesn't seem worthy of the extra £9,000 you need to spend over the Barchetta'. Bob Harper complained that 'on the road it doesn't feel quite as brisk as the figures suggest . . . it sounds faster than it is . . . [and] we did have a few nervous overtaking moments when pressing on along the back roads.'

As for the handling and roadholding, 'rapid progress can certainly be maintained, but it's rather harder work than it should be.' Overall, the Z3's 'school report would certainly come into the could do better, must try harder category'.

The same magazine had already tested a UK-specification 3.0i roadster for its December 2000 issue, and writer Stuart Gallagher had admitted to a degree of trepidation before setting out with the car. The shortcomings of earlier Z3s had all been in the chassis department, and nothing here seemed to have changed (had he forgotten the wider rear track?). Only the engine was new.

The new engine, already much praised in other BMW applications, did not disappoint:

ABOVE RIGHT AND RIGHT: **Aftermarket tuners continued to produce their own accessories. For those who found BMW's own hardtop a little staid, Hamann Motorsport offered this attractive style, with twin 'bumps' in the roof that offered a little more headroom. There was even a version that resembled carbon fibre.**

THE Z3, 2000–2002

> ### THE QUARTER-MILLIONTH Z3 ROADSTER
>
> The roadster was always a vastly more popular car than the coupé version of the Z3, and on 2 December 2001 the 250,000th example left the assembly line at Spartanburg. The car was painted Jet Black and had a red soft top. The seats were in Mugello Red with black inserts, and the console was trimmed with red birchwood. The rollover bars were trimmed with black leather in front and red leather behind, the two sections being joined by red stitching.

> *From as low as 2,000rpm you feel there is nothing this motor isn't happy doing. . . . With every maximum revs change up you are delivered slap bang in the middle of the engine's sweet spot, with another hedonistic attack on the horizon never more than a flex of your right foot away. The sound track is just as intoxicating.*

Nevertheless, those initial concerns proved well-founded. 'The Z3 falls down when it comes to involvement . . . struggling to send the right messages back to the helm.' With unprogressive brakes, a choppy ride and noticeable scuttle shake, it disappointed Stuart Gallagher.

> *At anything other than ten-tenths, the Z3 is all at sea, swaying from apex to apex with little control and the Dynamic Stability Control blinking furiously as it stamps its authority on proceedings . . . this was the only way to extract the small levels of ability from the Z3 – driving like a complete hooligan.*

So the new M54 engine was not enough to redeem earlier models of Z3.

> *The Z3 remains, in our opinion, a thorn in BMW's side. Yes, it's a sales success, has fans all over the world . . . and commands a three month waiting list should you order one today. But there is something about the diminutive BMW roadster which fails to get our juices flowing . . . the Z3 has its heart in the right place, but it has no soul.*

> ### Z3 PAINT OPTIONS, 2000–2002 MODELS
>
> **2000 model year**
>
> | *Colour/BMW code* | *Colour/BMW code* |
> |---|---|
> | Alpine White 300 | Impala Brown metallic 418 |
> | Bright Red 314 | Jet Black 668 |
> | Cosmos Black metallic 303 | Oxford Green metallic 430 |
> | Dakar Yellow 337 | Siena Red metallic 362 |
> | Estoril Blue metallic 335 | Steel Grey metallic 400 |
> | Evergreen metallic 358 | Titanium Silver metallic 354 |
> | Imola Red metallic 405 | Topaz Blue metallic 364 |
>
> **2001 model year**
>
> | *Colour/BMW code* | *Colour/BMW code* |
> |---|---|
> | Alpine White 300 | Jet Black 668 |
> | Atlanta Blue metallic 306 | Oxford Green metallic 430 |
> | Bright Red 314 | Siena Red metallic 362 |
> | Cosmos Black metallic 303 | Steel Grey metallic 400 |
> | Dakar Yellow 337 | Titanium Silver metallic 354 |
> | Impala Brown metallic 418 | Topaz Blue metallic 364 |
>
> **2002 model year**
>
> | *Colour/BMW code* | *Colour/BMW code* |
> |---|---|
> | Alpine White 300 | Oxford Green metallic 430 |
> | Atlanta Blue metallic 306 | Pistachio Green metallic 468 |
> | Black Sapphire metallic 475 | Siena Red metallic 362 |
> | Bright Red 314 | Sterling Grey metallic 472 |
> | Dakar Yellow 337 | Titanium Silver metallic 354 |
> | Impala Brown metallic 418 | Topaz Blue metallic 364 |
> | Jet Black 668 | |

Autocar also tried a 3.0i roadster for its issue dated 21 February 2001, and came to much the same conclusions. The magazine loved the new engine,

> *but its refinement only serves to highlight the shortcomings of the Z3's chassis. For a car designed to be roofless there's an alarming amount of scuttle shake . . . [and] it influences the car's ride and handling. . . . There's more lean and bounce than you'd expect in such an explicitly sporting car and this robs you of the confidence you need fully to exploit the glorious engine.*

THE Z3, 2000–2002

The magazine concluded that 'at £26,930 the Z3 3.0 compares well with other fun but flawed roadsters like the Audi TT and Honda S2000. If the chassis matched the engine it would blow them into the weeds.'

The 2002 Model Year

By the time the 2002 model year opened in the autumn of 2001, most buyers knew that a 'new' Z3 would be not long in coming. The relatively small number of what marketing specialists like to call 'product actions' for the 2002 model year Z3 was therefore not very surprising. Perhaps the most notable was that an in-dash CD player became part of the standard specification.

The very last Z3 left the assembly line at Spartanburg on 28 June 2002 (at 12.34pm, according to BMW). It was a 6-cylinder roadster in Sepia metallic paint with an Arizona Sun leather interior, and was retained at Spartanburg for display in the Zentrum museum and visitor centre. Not known for missing an opportunity, BMW press managers pointed out in the press release about the car that production of the next-generation BMW roadster would begin that autumn. And so indeed it did.

Z3 SPECIFICATIONS, 2000–2002 MODELS

Engines

1.8-litre
Type M43B18 4-cylinder petrol
1895cc (83.5 × 85mm)
Single ohc, chain-driven
2v per cylinder
Five-bearing crankshaft
Compression ratio 9.7:1
BMS46 engine management system
Three-way catalytic converter standard
116PS (118bhp) at 5,500rpm
168Nm (133lb ft) at 3,900rpm

2.0-litre
Type M52B20 6-cylinder petrol
1991cc (80 × 66mm)
Twin ohc, chain-driven
4v per cylinder
Double-VANOS variable valve timing
Seven-bearing crankshaft
Compression ratio 11.0:1
M42.0 engine management system giving sequential port injection
Three-way catalytic converter standard

152PS (150bhp) at 5,900rpm
190Nm (140lb ft) at 3,500rpm

2.2-litre
Type M54B22 6-cylinder petrol
2171cc (80 × 72mm)
Twin ohc, chain-driven
4v per cylinder
Double-VANOS variable valve timing
Seven-bearing crankshaft
Compression ratio 10.8:1
MS43.0 engine management system giving sequential port injection
Three-way catalytic converter standard
170PS (168bhp) at 6,100rpm
210Nm (155lb ft) at 3,500rpm

2.3-litre
Type M52B25 6-cylinder petrol
2494cc (84 × 75mm)
Twin ohc, chain-driven
4v per cylinder

(continued overleaf...)

(continued from previous page)

Double-VANOS variable valve timing
Seven-bearing crankshaft
Compression ratio 10.5:1
Bosch Motronic engine management system giving sequential port injection
Three-way catalytic converter standard
170PS (168bhp) at 5,500rpm
245Nm (181lb ft) at 3,500rpm

2.5-litre
Type M54B25 six-cylinder petrol
2494cc (84 x 75mm)
Twin overhead camshafts, chain-driven
Four valves per cylinder
Double-VANOS variable valve timing
Seven-bearing crankshaft
Compression ratio 10.5:1
Siemens engine management system
Three-way catalytic converter standard
184bhp at 6,000rpm
175lb ft at 3,500rpm

2.8-litre
Type M52B28 6-cylinder petrol
2793cc (84 x 84mm)
Twin ohc, chain-driven
4v per cylinder
Double-VANOS variable valve timing
Seven-bearing crankshaft
Compression ratio 10.2:1
Siemens engine management system
Three-way catalytic converter standard
European engines:
193PS (190bhp) at 5,500rpm
280Nm (210lb ft) at 3,500rpm
North American engines:
189bhp at 5,300rpm
203lb ft at 3,950rpm

3.0-litre
Type M54B30 6-cylinder petrol
2979cc (84 x 89.6mm)
Twin ohc, chain-driven
4v per cylinder
Double-VANOS variable valve timing
Seven-bearing crankshaft
Compression ratio 10.2:1

MS43.0 engine management system giving sequential port injection
Three-way catalytic converter standard
230PS (228bhp) at 5,900rpm
300Nm (221lb ft) at 3,500rpm

Transmission
Five-speed ZF manual gearbox standard
    Ratios 4.23:1, 2.53:1, 1.66:1, 1.22:1, 1.00:1 (1.8, 2.0 and 2.2i)
    Ratios 4.20:1, 2.49:1, 1.66:1, 1.24:1, 1.00:1 (2.3, 2.8 and 3.0i)
Four-speed ZF automatic gearbox optional, 1.8 and 2.0 models only
    Ratios 2.40:1, 1.47:1, 1.00:1, 0.72:1
Five-speed ZF automatic gearbox with AGS optional, 2.2i, 2.5i and 3.0i
    Ratios 3.42:1, 2.52:1, 1.61:1, 1.00:1, 0.75:1

Axle ratio
3.07:1   (3.0i manual)
3.15:1   (2.3 and 2.8 manual, 3.0i automatic)
3.38:1   (2.2i manual)
3.45:1   (1.8 and 2.0 manual; 2.2i automatic)
3.46:1   (2.5i manual)

Suspension, steering and brakes
Front suspension with MacPherson struts, lower L-arms and anti-roll bar
Rear suspension with semi-trailing arms, separate springs and dampers, and anti-roll bar
Rack-and-pinion steering with 16.8:1 ratio (1.8 models) or 13.9:1 ratio (2.0, 2.2i, 2.3, 2.5i and 3.0i models) and standard power assistance
Disc brakes all round, twin hydraulic circuits; ABS standard. 286mm (11.26in) front discs, and 280mm (11in) rear discs

Dimensions
Overall length   4,050mm (159.4in)
Overall width   1,740mm (68.5in)
Overall height   1,288mm (50.7in)
Wheelbase   2,446mm (96.3in)
Front track   1,418mm (55.8in)
Rear track   1,431mm (56.3in)

(continued opposite...)

(continued from opposite page)

Wheels and tyres
7J x 16 five-spoke alloy wheels, with 225/50 ZR 16 tyres standard
7.5J x 17 front and 8.5J x 17 rear alloy wheels with 225/50 ZR 17 and 245/40 ZR 17 tyres optional

Unladen weights
2.0 Roadster	1,270kg (2,800lb)		
2.2i Roadster	1,345kg (2,965lb) with manual gearbox		
	1,385kg (3,053lb) with automatic gearbox		
2.3 Roadster	1,315kg (2,899lb) with manual gearbox		
			1,355kg (2,987lb) with automatic gearbox
2.8 Roadster			1,260kg (2,778lb)
2.8 Roadster (US)			1,320kg (2,910lb) with manual gearbox
			1,360kg (2,998lb) with automatic gearbox
2.8 Coupé			1,300kg (2,866lb)
3.0i			1,360kg (2,998lb) with manual gearbox
			1,400kg (3,086lb) with automatic gearbox

Z3 PERFORMANCE FIGURES, 2000–2002 MODELS

'1.8' Roadster	0–60mph	10.0sec
	Maximum	122mph (196km/h)
2.0 Roadster	0–60mph	8.5sec
	Maximum	131mph (210km/h)
2.2i Roadster	0–60mph	7.6sec
	Maximum	139mph (224km/h)
2.5i Roadster	0–60mph	6.7sec
	Maximum	128mph (206km/h)
2.8 Roadster	0–60mph	6.6sec
	Maximum	144mph (231km/h)
3.0i Roadster	0–60mph	5.8sec
	Maximum	149mph (240km/h)
3.0i Coupé	0–60mph	5.8sec
	Maximum	155mph (250km/h)

■ THE Z3, 2000–2002

VINS AND PRODUCTION DATES FOR Z3 MAINSTREAM MODELS, 1996–2002

Z3 1.8

All were European-specification roadsters. The first six cars were pre-production prototypes.

LA59000–59005	12/94	6	
LA59006–88851	2/95–9/98	29,846	**29,852**

Z3 1.9 (and later Z3 1.8)
All were roadsters.

European specification

LA14000–44418	04/95–04/99	30,419	
LB01000–05216	7/95–4/97	4,217	
LD10000–13078	09/97–03/99	3,079	
LD80000–85991	04/97–08/98	5,992	
LD86120–88182	08/98–04/99	2,063	
LF00000–23335	01/98–06/02	23,336	
LG23000–25998	09/98–07/01	2,999	**72,105**

US specification (all badged as Z3 1.9)

LB65001–84999	7/95–4/97	19,999	
LD15000–17169	09/97–08/98	2,170	
LE00700–00799	04/96	100	
LE01000–09878	04/97–04/98	8,879	**31,148**

(LE00700–00799 were the special 100-strong 007 Edition cars.)

Total, 1.9-litre cars   103,253

Z3 2.0

All were European-specification roadsters.

LG16000–16763	07/98–10/00	764	
LG26000–34181	08/98–09/00	8,182	
LG71000–73979	09/98–10/00	2,980	
LG84000–86687	09/98–09/00	2,688	**14,614**

Z3 2.2i

All were European-specification roadsters.

LK00000–07012	12/99–06/02	7,013	
LK15000–17488	02/00–06/02	2,489	
LL72000–74643	01/00–06/02	2,644	**12,146**

Z3 2.3

All were US-specification roadsters.

LF79000–92775	01/98–08/00	13,776	
LG00000–05999	02/98–12/99	6,000	
LG18000–18999	03/99–03/00	1,000	
LM91000–92715	03/00–08/00	1,716	**22,492**

Z3 2.5i

All were US-specification roadsters.

LK45000–49887	01/00–09/01	4,888	
LK51000–52731	09/01–06/02	1,732	
LM00000–04389	02/00–09/01	4,390	
LM05000–07129	09/01–06/02	2,130	**13,140**

Z3 2.8

Roadsters

European specification

LB08000–08827	09/97–08/98	828	
LD40000–50768	08/96–08/98	10,769	
LE61000–65783	05/98–05/00	4,784	
LE86000–86789	01/98–05/00	790	
LE91000–93420	03/98–05/00	2,421	**19,592**

US specification

LB62000–62841	9/97–12/97	842	
LB63061–63999	2/98–5/98	939	

(continued opposite...)

(continued from opposite page)

LC00100–16358	8/96–9/98	16,259	
LF40001–44552	01/98–05/00	4,552	
LF70000–72188	03/98–05/00	2,189	
LG20000–20708	05/98–09/98	709	**25,490**

South African specification

LB85000–89410	01/97–08/98	4,411	**4,411**

Total 2.8-litre roadsters 49,493

Coupés

European specification

LC98000–99294	01/98–05/00	1,295	
LD55000–56471	06/97–08/98	1,472	
LG06000–14047	04/98–08/98	8,048	**10,815**

US specification

LE95000–95882	04/98–12/99	883	**883**

Total 2.8-litre coupés 11,698

Combined total, European specification 2.8-litre 30,407
Combined total, US-specification 2.8-litre 26,373
Total, South African 2.8-litre 4,411
Grand total, 2.8-litre models 61,191

Z3 3.0i

Roadsters

European specification

LJ25000–28385	09/99–06/02	3,386	
LJ40000–41440	09/99–06/02	1,441	
LL20000–20998	09/99–06/02	999	
LL33000–33763	09/99–06/02	764	
LL60000–60286	12/01–06/02	287	**6,877**

US specification

LJ55000–61170	10/99–06/02	6,171	
LL46000–51131	09/99–06/02	5,132	**11,303**

Total 3.0i roadsters 18,180

Coupés

European specification

LJ00000–02173	10/99–06/02	2,174	
LL95000–95546	09/99–09/01	547	**2,721**

US specification

LJ15000–16135	09/99–04/02	1,136	
LM13000–14093	09/99–04/02	1,094	**2,230**

Total 3.0i coupés 4,951

Combined total, European specification 3.0i 9,598
Combined total, US specification 3.0i 13,533
Grand total, 3.0i models 23,131

All-model totals

Z3 1.8	29,852
Z3 1.9	103,253
Z3 2.0	14,614
Z3 2.2i	12,146
Z3 2.3	35,632
Z3 2.8	61,191
Z3 3.0i	23,131
Grand total	***279,819***

European specification	168,722
South African specification	4,411
US specification	106,686
Grand total	***279,819***

CHAPTER FOUR

THE M DIVISION'S Z3

Even though the Z3 had been drawn up as an affordable roadster, the idea that BMW should create an expensive very high-performance derivative through its M division can never have been far away. This was certainly not a betrayal of the original concept; it was simply an enhancement of it. The M division – previously known as the Motorsport division, which had been set up initially to facilitate BMW's racing programme in the 1960s and 1970s – specialized in creating high-performance versions of the company's everyday cars. Products such as the M3 and M5 saloons had been proven to have a halo effect on sales of the more mundane models on which they were based.

The transformation of the Z3 was not going to be too difficult to achieve. It had been designed to accommodate BMW's M52 2.8-litre 6-cylinder engine, and this very design was already being developed as the engine for the Evolution version of the E36 M3 that would be introduced in 1996. For a variety of reasons, but primarily to meet emissions regulations, there were to be two different M division 6-cylinders with the same 3.2-litre swept volume. There would be considerable differences between the European-specification S50B32 and the US-specification S52B32US.

Obviously, putting the huge power and torque of one of these engines into the Z3 was going to call for changes to the chassis, and the M division had probably begun work on those changes before the roadster even entered production in South Carolina. Much of the necessary hardware already existed: the rear suspension of the Z3 was essentially that of the E30 3 Series cars and so the uprated components used

Although yellow seems to predominate in the cars illustrated in this chapter, it was just one of several special colours available for the M cars. The keen sculpting of the front apron and side sills is clear in this picture of an M Roadster, as is the special wing vent with its discreet M badge.

THE M DIVISION'S Z3

BMW had used every trick in the book to make the cockpit of the M Roadster special and, as this picture shows, the result was a great success. The two-tone leather added an upmarket feel and the additional instruments on the centre console added a more sporty one. Even the oval rear-view mirror was special.

in the E30 M3 were already available. The rest of the suspension was shared with the E36 models, and the brakes could be borrowed from the planned E36 M3 Evo cars – although there would be a wrinkle in this plan before production began.

The M division's cars were also expected to have cosmetic differences from the everyday models, so work was put in hand to achieve those as well. For enthusiasts of the M cars, there was and still is a special thrill in the detail touches that distinguish these models, and BMW's designers knew they had to deliver on that level.

Meanwhile, there was another factor driving development of the M division's Z3s. BMW marketing has often depended on building anticipation of new models by revealing them in concept form a year or more before they actually become available through the showrooms. So what the company called an M Roadster was shown as a concept car at the Geneva Motor Show in March 1996, less than six months after the basic Z3 had been introduced. The car's special red and black interior helped it to gain plenty of press attention even if this preview was a little overshadowed by the world premiere of the Jaguar XK8 coupé at the same show. In practice, however, no cars would become available until nearly a year later. And that was just in Europe; the North American version would not reach showrooms until March 1998.

The European M Roadsters

BMW knew all versions of the M Roadster as E36/7 types, using the same code as for the basic Z3 roadster. The cars were assembled in South Carolina alongside the mainstream Z3s, although their special drivetrains were shipped from the M division in Germany.

Production of the European M Roadsters actually began in September 1996, and the cars were introduced to the press in March 1997 in the mountains of southern Spain. Those who attended had a chance to sample their performance at the old Jerez Grand Prix circuit. Actual sales began in Europe a couple of months later, but only of cars with left-hand drive; these had the CK91 specification. Right-hand-drive Britain had to wait until the start of 1998 to get cars (which became CK92 types), and the USA had to wait even longer to get its own special version of the M Roadster.

The big news about the M Roadster was of course its 3.2-litre S50 engine. This was a further development of the iron-block, aluminium-head, four-valve 3.0-litre type that had been introduced in 1992 for the E36 M3, and it would also find its way into the 1996-model E36 M3 Evo. Unusually for BMW, it was an undersquare design, with an 86.4mm bore and a long 91mm stroke that gave 3201cc.

■ THE M DIVISION'S Z3

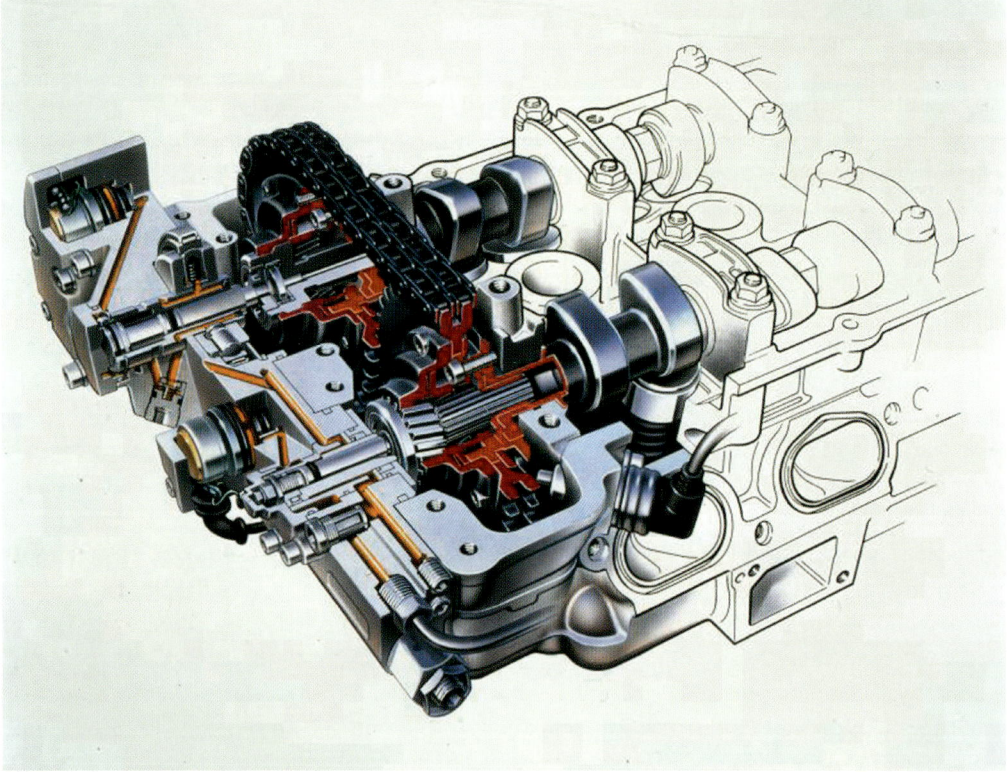

TOP AND BOTTOM: The hardware of the Double-VANOS system depended on electronic control software. These pictures show what the unit looked like on the engine, and what there was inside it.

The original 3.0-litre engine had a Single-VANOS variable valve timing system, which moved the inlet camshaft forwards or backwards in its housing hydraulically to provide different cam profiles, so optimizing valve timing at all speeds to give maximum bottom-end torque as well as top-end power. For the new 3.2-litre type, the engineers at the M division had developed this further to give variable control of both the inlet and exhaust camshafts, and the new system was known as Double-VANOS. This needed a powerful electronic control system, and the M division had developed a unique type in conjunction with specialists Siemens. It was called the MSS50 and boasted a computing power of 20 million instructions per second.

Other features of the engine were individual throttle plates for each cylinder, lightweight pistons and a high compression ratio of 11.3:1, enlarged inlet valves, a reworked exhaust manifold and graphite-coated conrods to reduce friction. A secondary oil pump pick-up guaranteed adequate lubrication when the car was cornering hard, and the smoothness expected of a BMW six was aided by an improved dual-mass flywheel and a modified vibration damper. All this combined to give 321PS (317bhp) at 7,400rpm and 258lb ft of torque at 3,250rpm. In a car as light as the Z3 Roadster, the promise was immediately obvious.

Even though the 3.2-litre engine had been an obvious choice for the M Roadster, the M3 Evo's drivetrain could not be transplanted into the car without modification. In the M3, the 3.2-litre engine was to be accompanied by a new six-speed manual gearbox, but this was physically too large to fit into the more confined space available in the Z3. So the M division's engineers had to use the older five-speed ZF Type C gearbox instead.

This very special drivetrain put its power to the rear wheels through a 3.15:1 final drive, taller than in any other Z3 derivative. To prevent the car from breaking traction with irritating frequency, a limited-slip differential with a 25 per cent locking ratio was added as standard equipment. There were other changes to the suspension and brakes to make sure the extra power was not squandered.

Although the M Roadster retained the standard Z3 layout of MacPherson struts up front with semi-trailing arms at the rear, it had modified front suspension geometry, stronger semi-trailing arms, and a reinforced subframe. The ride height was reduced by just over an inch; there were wider tracks, thicker anti-roll bars, and stiffer springs and dampers. Brakes were taken straight from the E36 M3 of the time, and consisted of ventilated discs on all four wheels – with ABS as standard, of course. The brakes on the front wheels had two-piece construction that combined aluminium hubs with steel discs for better heat disspation, and were generally known as 'floating' types. Naturally, the M Roadster also came with wider wheels and tyres than the mainstream Z3 models. These wheels had a 17in diameter and wider rims at the rear to take fatter tyres that improved the car's grip when cornering. They were always of a five-spoke pattern known as the M RoadStar type and had a bright Chromeline finish.

All this was built into what was essentially the 6-cylinder Z3 bodyshell with its wide wheel arches. However, the M Roadster was distinguished by a special front apron that incorporated brake cooling ducts where the mainstream cars had fog lights; by special wing vents with bright horizontal trim and an M logo; by bullet-shaped M door mirrors; and, at a closer look, by chromed windscreen washer nozzles on the bonnet. At the rear, the bumper apron was lower down than on mainstream Z3s, with a shrouded central light for the number plate, now relocated between the tail lights. Finishing touches were two pairs of exhaust tailpipes and, of course, the M logo on the right. Inevitably, the M Roadster would be made available in paint colours not offered on the mainstream Z3s. Headlamp washers were made an optional fit, although they would not become available on North American cars.

As for the interior, it was bursting with the subtle touches so beloved of M enthusiasts. The main instruments had chrome bezels and red needles, and the face of the rev counter had an M logo. There were three auxiliary dials (a clock, an oil temperature gauge and an outside temperature gauge) on the centre console, all with matching chrome bezels. The steering wheel was a 375mm three-spoke M type with tri-colour stitching and colour-matched accents, and the gearshift grip was covered in leather and illuminated when the sidelights were on, with a chrome surround for its shroud and an M logo on the shift pattern guide.

Even the rear-view mirror was special, having a distinctive oval shape. The sports seats came with two-stage heating as standard and with special pleated leather upholstery that was available in all-black or with a two-tone finish. The door pulls and centre console were trimmed in Nappa leather, while the interior door handles were chromed and the sill plates each carried an M logo. Air conditioning was of course a standard fit, while cruise control was standard in some markets and optional in others. Various audio options were listed, the top one being a Harmon/Kardon system.

The North American M Roadsters

Production of the North American-specification M Roadster did not begin until February 1998, and this derivative was known as the CK93 type. Its biggest difference from the European-specification cars lay in its drivetrain, where the engine was only superficially similar to the European S50.

Although the North American engine was also described as a 3.2-litre type, it had completely different bore and stroke dimensions and a swept volume of 3152cc. BMW had adopted exactly the same engine strategy for the M Roadster as for the M3 Evo, which in North American form also had this smaller-capacity engine. The reasons were not entirely to do with emissions, as is commonly believed. They had more to do with fuel consumption: the US Corporate Average Fuel Economy (CAFE) regulations tilted the balance between performance and economy decisively towards the latter. Cars with poor fuel economy were subject to a 'gas guzzler' tax, which inflated their showroom prices and inevitably made them less saleable.

The S52B32US engine was another iron-block, alloy-head type with 4v per cylinder, but it was based much more closely on the production M52 small-block 6-cylinder. It also had VANOS variable valve timing only on the inlet camshaft, although this was specially tuned to give optimum power at high engine speeds. Despite a ported and polished cylinder head, heavy-duty valve springs, low-mass valve lifters, springs and spring seats, carefully balanced camshafts and special free-flow inlet and exhaust systems, it was very much down on its European equivalent. Quoted outputs were just 240bhp (to SAE standards) at 6,000rpm and 236lb ft of torque at 3,800rpm.

The S52 engine drove through the same five-speed gearbox as in the European models, but the North American cars were given a lower final drive than their European equivalents in order to maintain acceleration with the smaller engine. The scheme worked: BMW claimed 5.5sec for the 0–60mph sprint in a North American-specification M Roadster, which compared quite favourably with the 5.2sec claimed for its European equivalent. Top speed was admittedly a little lower at 137mph (220km/h) – but that was quite fast enough for a country that was then subject to a near-universal 55mph speed limit. It is also said that the North American cars had less soundproofing than the European models, to add a little aural excitement in the lower speed ranges as well as to reduce weight.

The suspension of the North American cars was the same as that of their European equivalents. Nevertheless, there was a difference in the brakes: just as on the M3 Evo models, US customers were denied the two-piece 'floating' front discs. The reason was simple: BMW of North America were afraid that these discs might fail if not properly maintained, and the risk of being sued was too great. In Canada, where customers were less litigation-happy, the M Roadster came with an essentially North American specification but with the two-piece front brake discs.

The North American cars had several differences in the exterior detail from their European equivalents. The most obvious was that they featured amber side marker lights in the front bumper apron. They also had 'free-form' headlights in place of the ellipsoid type fitted to the European cars, and as the single rear number-plate light did not meet US regulations, in its place came a light on either side of the plate. Cars for Canada had the addition of daytime-running lights and could also be fitted optionally with the headlamp washers denied to US customers.

There were differences inside, too: where the European cars had a 170mph speedometer and a rev counter redlined at 7,200rpm, the North American cars had a 160mph speedometer and a rev counter with a redline graduated between 6,500 and 7,000rpm to suit the variable redline of the S52 engine. On the centre console, the first North American cars had a deactivation switch for the passenger's side airbag in the central position instead of the outside temperature gauge fitted to European cars. Later, this was replaced by a voltmeter, and dealers would upgrade early cars to the later specification if owners so requested.

What the Press Thought

Surprising though it may seem today, the UK motoring press were not very enthusiastic about the new M Roadster. Their criticisms focused on two main areas. The first was that there was no disguising the car's humble origins in the Z3, and the second was that it was not very exciting to drive.

Autocar seemed in two minds about the car after testing one for its issue dated 28 January 1998. On the one hand, it provided 'exactly the fillip that the Z3 needs... . The M Roadster is the genuine article, a hairy-chested hot rod complete with over-inflated wheel arches, engine

The M Roadster was visually sharpened by a number of cosmetic changes from the mainstream cars, but there was a strong argument that it did not look different enough from them.

This UK-market M Roadster at rest shows two of the M Roadster's unique features. One is the deeper front spoiler with its more aggressive air intakes and the other is the special wheels with their 'chromed' finish.

and, of course, price.' On the other hand, the testers summarized the new BMW as 'a brutally fast but uninvolving sports car'.

Certainly, they admitted, it was the fastest-accelerating BMW production model yet. The 0–60mph sprint took just 5.1sec, which was actually 0.1sec faster than the traditionally conservative claim from its makers. Its road behaviour was superb, and 'even the most hardened drivers cannot fail to be impressed by its astonishing brakes, performance and grip'. As for the suspension changes, 'these raise the M Roadster's handling onto a different plane from other Z3s'.

The other side of the story was that there was too much body shimmy and the steering was neither fast nor precise enough. Equally, 'there is no getting away from the limitations of its comparatively flexible chassis'. The driving position was rather cramped for tall drivers, and some form of steering column adjustment would have been welcome. But perhaps the biggest problem for the *Autocar* team was that the car lacked the appeal of rivals like the Porsche Boxster or Lotus Elise: 'It doesn't feel as special as a purpose-built machine like a TVR.'

Those impressions were still colouring the *Autocar* view of the car in a later issue.

> The M Roadster should have been an instant classic. . . . In the event, it was just quick. There was no edge, no finesse, no intimacy. But quite a lot of body shake over bumps. A half-decent hot rod, then, but not subtle or satisfying enough to be a top-drawer sports car.

When the US motoring magazines published their first opinions a couple of months later, there was a similar mixed reaction. *Automobile Magazine* for March 1998 described the M Roadster as 'a hale and hairy sports car, easily the most exciting of the Z3 variants, with handling that invites – rather than discourages – mass exploitation of 240 innocent horsepower'. The magazine was content to quote BMW North America's claim of a 5.5sec 0–60mph time, and did not question the M Roadster's performance credentials. However, something seemed to be missing. Writer Jamie Kitman targeted BMW's claim to build the Ultimate Driving Machine, complaining that the car was 'something less than the ultimate driving machine'. The problem was an excess of refinement – the same problem then affecting views of the 6-cylinder M3 saloons which had lost the rorty appeal of the 4-cylinder original.

Car and Driver magazine, also dated March 1998, ran the M Roadster against the latest Chevrolet Corvette roadster and a Porsche Boxster. The M Roadster could only achieve second place in a close-run contest with the lower-powered (201bhp) Porsche. The suspension proved its biggest weakness, allowing too much body roll, too much squat under acceleration and too much dive under braking. In addition, the BMW scored poorly on features and amenities, although it was awarded the same ten fun-to-drive points as the Porsche.

Road & Track, again dated March 1998, was rather more positive and its testers clearly enjoyed their time with the M Roadster. They recorded just 5.2sec for the 0–60mph sprint, noting that this was the fastest-accelerating BMW ever sold in the USA and that it had 'phenomenal acceleration'. The driver could induce power oversteer if he felt so inclined but, on the whole, 'this is a well-built weekend car that's refined enough to drive every day'. The US showroom price included free maintenance for 36,000 miles or three years and, the magazine summarized, 'your smiles are guaranteed to last a lot longer'.

Production Changes, 1997–2001

Even though the M Roadsters were very fully equipped from the beginning and could be ordered with a variety of specifications to suit individual tastes, BMW made a number of changes to them as production went on.

The original six-colour paint palette was increased to seven colours in December 1997 (see the table at the end of this Chapter), but nothing more changed before September 1998. By this time, feedback from the first North American customers had become available, and in fact some changes were specific to the North American-specification cars. These now gained ASC + T traction control for the 1999 model year, along with the option of a BMW Business RDS CD radio system. Another new option, this time for most of the markets where the M Roadster was sold, was side-impact airbags. A further shuffle of paint and trim options brought two additional exterior paints and one additional interior combination.

A second set of changes, introduced in April 1999, again brought only minor differences. The M Roadster's appearance was sharpened by adding chrome headlight surrounds and chrome slats to the radiator grilles. The central locking was extended to include the fuel filler flap, the airbags were

THE M DIVISION'S Z3

THE CANADIAN SPECIAL EDITION

The only special edition of the M Roadster was made available in Canada during the 2000 model year. This drew on options from the BMW Individual range and consisted of twelve cars painted in Velvet Blue metallic from the BMW Individual range. Their interiors were upholstered in BMW Individual Ink Blue + Black Nappa leather, and featured a bi-coloured Ink Blue + Black M steering wheel.

changed for two-stage 'smart' versions, and the insulation of the convertible top was improved. There were more paint revisions, as the silver and green metallic options changed.

Just three months later, in July 1999, came an upgrade for the optional Harmon/Kardon audio system. There would then be no more changes until August 2000, when the paint palette was pruned. Although other Z3 Roadsters took on new rear wings and rear lights for the 2000 model year, the M Roadsters did not. The reason was quite simple: a number of bodyshells had been set aside in anticipation of orders for the M models, and these old-style shells had to be used up.

M Coupé, 1998

The North American market had not even received its first M Roadsters when BMW previewed the M Coupé at the Frankfurt Motor Show in September 1997. However, this was a typical BMW 'tease': production would not begin until April 1998 for Europe; North American-specification cars followed in July and the first right-hand-drive European-specification cars were built in August 1998.

The M Coupé shared its bodyshell with the 6-cylinder version of the mainstream Z3 coupé, although like the M Roadster it had a different boot floor to accommodate the battery and make room for the paired dual exhausts. It also shared with the M Roadster the front apron with brake cooling ducts and the restyled tail with its number plate mounted high up between the light clusters. Special side vents, chromed washer jets and bullet-shaped door mirrors were also the same as on the M Roadsters. The North American cars again followed the lead of the M Roadsters, with amber side marker lights, 'free form' headlights and twin rear number-plate lights to distinguish them from the European models.

The car shared all of its running gear with the M Roadster, and there were European-specification models with the S50 engine and North American types with the lower-powered S52 type. However, coupés had stiffer springs and dampers than roadsters, probably to compensate for the greater weight of the bodyshell. It appears that a sharper steering

The Coupé was no more attractive in its **M** form than as a mainstream 6-cylinder model, but the M addenda did add a certain stylish brutality to its appearance. This is a UK-market car, at its best in Imola Red paint.

■ THE M DIVISION'S Z3

Like the M Roadster, the M Coupé had distinctive pairs of exhaust tailpipes. This is another UK-market car, this time in attention-grabbing Estoril Blue metallic.

This cutaway drawing was issued at the launch of the M Coupé, and shows the layout of the car well. The engine is an S50 or S52 unit.

rack had been tried during development but did not make it onto the production cars. Not surprisingly, the M Coupé's interior trim was the same as in its Roadster sibling, although there was a 'Coupé' logo at the bottom of the rev counter and of course the load bay had its own special trim.

M Coupés could be bought with the same options as their M Roadster contemporaries, although the paint palette differed slightly. There were also a few special items. An electrically operated glass sunroof was available, as were a rear partition net and load bay cover. For the first two years of the model's availability, changes to the Coupé paralleled those listed above for the Roadster.

THE M DIVISION'S Z3

What the Press Thought

The styling of the coupé brought some criticism, as it had done for the mainstream derivatives, but those who tested an M Coupé for motoring magazines welcomed the improvements that the stiffer bodyshell made to the handling. The biggest criticism echoed one that had been made of the Roadster, which was that its 51ltr (11gal) fuel tank was too small for a car that drank fuel as fast as this one did. BMW's engineers responded that they would have liked to install a larger tank, but that to do so would have required a re-engineered floorpan, which would have been too costly for the likely sales volumes.

In Britain, where the M Coupé was initially the only Z3 derivative available with the coupé bodyshell, *Autocar* magazine was quite ecstatic about the car. The test team found it 'an altogether more capable and enjoyable driving machine' than the M Roadster. 'Crucial to this improvement is body rigidity – it's more than double the roadster's. . . . A stiff structure means the elimination of bump steer, far greater refinement and a quality to the driving that's completely lacking in the roadster.' Performance also proved to be better, with a 0–60mph time of just 4.9sec and a maximum of 160mph – despite the speed limiter. In fact, the magazine claimed to have seen 165mph on a derestricted Autobahn in Germany, and noted that very high speeds were achievable not only on motorways: 'Across country,' enthused a later *Autocar* evaluation, 'the M is terrifically, insanely fast.'

Perfect it was not, however, and it was not only the M Coupé's looks that were flawed. Even though it was 'a more convincing driving machine' than the M Roadster, it was

> one that still lacks the fluency, precision and delicacy of a great sports car . . . too cramped and compromised to be a GT, too detached and anodyne to be the back-to-basics thrill-seeker promised by its maker. What we are left with is an eccentricity which, engine and blistering performance apart, is more style than substance.

In practice, the M Coupé would never be a strong seller in Britain.

M Roadster and M Coupé, 2001–2002

The next evolution of the M Roadster and M Coupé was influenced by requirements elsewhere in the M division's product range. The E36 M3 had gone out of production in mid-1998 (although convertible production continued at a low level and primarily for the US market until December 1999) and a new M3 based on the latest E46 3 Series models was due for introduction in autumn 2000. With it would come a new engine, and that new engine would go into the M Roadster and M Coupé as well, just as soon as production levels had built up.

In practice, the first Z3 derivatives with the new engine were not built until February 2001, as initial engine supplies were all allocated to the hugely anticipated new M3. In the meantime, production of the M Roadsters and M Coupés had stopped over the summer of 2000, no doubt to allow dealers to sell the last of the old-stock models before the new ones became available. So supplies of these cars thinned out towards the end of the year and a reduced range of colours was on offer. However, BMW kept momentum going by announcing the new models at the Greater Los Angeles Auto Show in January 2001.

Having two different engines in production for the M derivatives of the Z3 had been an unwelcome complication for BMW, even though the E36 M3 had shared the same two engines. So a key aim was to develop a common design that would suit both European and North American markets with minimal modifications. The solution was an engine known as the S54 type, which was a further development of the S50 iron-block 'small six' seen in the E36 M3 and in European M Roadsters and M Coupés built before summer 2000. Still described as a 3.2-litre, it actually had a slightly larger swept volume of 3246cc thanks to a larger bore than the earlier engine. The cylinder head was again made of aluminium, but this time cast as a single piece in order to save weight; the compression ratio was also raised, to 11.5:1. Finger-type rocker arms reduced both reciprocating mass and friction, and the camshafts were modified. There was now a high-pressure Double VANOS system, capable of varying the valve timing continuously and of doing so more quickly at high engine revolutions.

The engine management system was new, too, once again developed jointly by BMW and Siemens and this time known as the MSS54 type. The six independent throttle bodies used on most engines from the M division were this time elec-

79

■ THE M DIVISION'S Z3

The later M Roadster and M Coupé had the S54 engine, which brought the power and torque figures of North American cars almost up to those for the European models.

tronically operated, and this made possible two M Dynamic Driving Control response modes. Most people referred to this system as a drive-by-wire type. The S54 engine also had a scavenging oil pump to reduce the risk of oil starvation under hard cornering.

Very noticeable to anyone familiar with the old engine was that this one revved higher: it was redlined at 8,000rpm and delivered its maximum power just 100rpm lower down the rev counter. It was also massively powerful, and on its introduction for the M3 in autumn 2000 BMW boasted that it had the highest specific output of any naturally aspirated engine they had ever made, with the exception of the V12 developed for the McLaren F1 supercar. For the M Roadster and M Coupé, it boasted 321bhp in European trim – not quite as much as in the M3 because of the Z3-based cars' more restrictive exhaust system but still slightly more than for the outgoing S50 engine.

The real improvement was for the North American cars, however, where the engine's 315bhp (320PS) rating represented a massive improvement over the 240bhp of the outgoing type. The North American figure was lower than the European one because the exhaust catalysts had to be relocated nearer the engine speed warm-up and so improve cold-start emissions on these cars, and this hindered the flow of the exhaust gases.

Maximum power figures were less relevant than they might have seemed on paper, of course, because BMW still subscribed to the German manufacturers' agreement and fitted all cars with a limiter that capped the maximum speed at 250km/h (155mph). That was quite fast enough for road use anywhere in the world, but the limiter could be removed by special request. As for torque, the S54 engine may have delivered its maximum torque of 350Nm (258lb ft) at higher revs than the engine it replaced, but there was more than enough of it at lower speeds to retain the brutal acceleration associated with the M division's versions of the Z3.

Under the bonnet, not a lot looked different from before. But where the earlier S50 and S52 engines had carried a 'BMW M Power' legend on their cam covers, the new S54 carried only a large letter M. As for the gearbox, there was no change, and the re-engined M Roadster and M Coupé both still came with the five-speed ZF Type C. European and North American versions both shared the same 3.15:1 final drive and, as before, a 25 per cent limited-slip differential was standard on all cars.

However, an innovation was BMW's Dynamic Stability Control (DSC) system, which replaced the earlier ASC + T system on North American models. The M Roadsters for

2001 now took on the stiffer suspension of the M Coupé, and all models were fitted with a tyre pressure monitoring system as standard.

Some cosmetic changes were only to be expected, but it was interesting that the new S54-engined cars still did not take on the revised rear wings and tail lights that had been introduced on the mainstream Z3 models in 1999. Clearly, the supply of bodyshells set aside for the M division had been enough to see them right through to the anticipated end of production. So, new paint colours apart, there were just two features that distinguished the new models from their forebears. One was a darker, Chrome Shadow finish for the wheels (which remained five-spoke M RoadStar types), and the other was a subtle curvature to the M badges on the bodywork, as seen on the latest M3 and M5 models. A small detail was that the M badge on the tail was mounted closer to the light unit than on earlier cars.

Not much was new on the inside, either. The instrument faces did differ, though, with a grey background and different graphics, and the North American models now shared a 170mph speedometer with the European cars. The rev counter was marked with a 7,600rpm redline, and an outside temperature gauge on the centre console was now standard for all markets. The North American cars also gained a smaller rear-view mirror with an auto-dimming function and a chrome frame.

What the Press Thought of the S54 Models

By the time the S54 engine was transplanted into the M Roadster and M Coupé, the models were barely newsworthy as far as the mainstream press was concerned. So despite the big gains in performance from the new engine (especially for North American cars), not a lot was written about them.

In the USA, both *Road & Track* magazine (December 2001) and *Motor Trend* magazine (April 2002) ran comparison tests between the M Roadster and its natural rival from Mercedes-Benz, the SLK 32 AMG. Both concluded that the BMW had the edge. *Road & Track* noted that the focus of the two cars was different: 'The M Roadster edges towards catering for the weekend racer, while the SLK 32 AMG takes a more civilized approach.' *Motor Trend* concluded that 'we'll give the M Roadster the trophy for offering more of the critical elements we feel constitute the ultimate roadster formula'.

Special colours were always a feature of the M cars, although more sober options were available as well. This right-hand-drive Coupé was finished in Dakar Yellow.

■ THE M DIVISION'S Z3

An M Coupé being used as intended – around a hill-climb course in the UK. MAGIC CAR PICS

THE SOUTH AFRICAN S54 M COUPÉS

South Africa took around 40 of the 165 right-hand-drive M Coupés with S54 engines, and the local importer prepared these specially. All of them were given a number of items from the AC Schnitzer aftermarket catalogue: suspension, exhaust, a short shift kit, special shift grip and 18in Type III wheels.

Epilogue

Sales of the M Roadster and M Coupé slowed down very noticeably after the S54-engined cars were introduced in early 2001, and it is not hard to understand why. The E46 M3 had become the focus of M enthusiasts' interest after its introduction in autumn 2000 and, although the new two-seaters were undoubtedly better cars than their immediate predecessors, they did not have the draw of the iconic M3.

A few figures will show exactly what was happening. In its first four years, the M Roadster had sold well over 3,300 examples a year, but sales in its final fifteen months worked out at around 1,530 a year. The M Coupé, never as much in demand, had sold nearly 2,600 copies a year for its first two years, but in those last fifteen months it sold just 1,112 cars, for an average of just under 890 cars in a year.

The final M Roadsters and M Coupés were built in May 2002, production of the right-hand-drive roadsters having ended a month earlier. Right through the production run of the M division's Z3 derivatives, right-hand-drive cars had been the least numerous and the North American-specification cars had always been the most plentiful. A grand total of 21,613 cars – 15,322 roadsters and 6,291 coupés – had carried M badges. The experiment would certainly be worth repeating, and BMW already had plans to do exactly that when the Z3's replacement model became available.

A LITTLE BIT MORE

As soon as the M Roadster became available, aftermarket tuners began to look at ways of increasing its performance. Although such modifications were always going to have a very limited appeal (not least because of their cost), there were always going to be a few customers who wanted to go a stage further than everybody else.

Typical of what became available was a conversion of the M Roadster and M Coupé available from Hartge. This was built around Hartge's own tuned versions of the BMW 4.4-litre V8 – initially in 4.7-litre (4722cc) form and later in a 5.0-litre size. The 4.7-litre engine produced 350bhp at 5,700rpm and 368.5lb ft of torque, and was harnessed to the six-speed gearbox that BMW insisted was too big to fit into the Z3 bodyshell. It gave performance of 0–100km/h (0–62mph) in 4.8sec with a top speed of 169mph (272km/h). Inevitably, Hartge also offered a number of cosmetic modifications for customers who wanted them.

In the USA, leading performance tuner Dinan developed a supercharged M Roadster that could accelerate to 60mph from rest in just 4.3sec and would reach 160mph (258km/h). This was a considerable achievement in view of the fact that the car was based on the lower-powered and lower-geared North American-specification model. Key to the Dinan conversion was a Vortech V2 supercharger with an intercooler, allied to a high-flow air intake system and larger injectors. Maximum power was quoted as 406bhp at 6,500rpm, with maximum torque of 333lb ft at 5,000rpm. The car was lowered on its suspension by means of shorter springs, and there were 22mm (0.87in) adjustable anti-roll bars front and rear. Like Hartge, Dinan also offered some cosmetic enhancements.

THE M DIVISION'S Z3

M ROADSTER PAINT OPTIONS

September 1996 to November 1997
Six paint colours were available:
Arctic Silver metallic 309   Cosmos Black metallic 303
Boston Green metallic 275   Estoril Blue metallic 335
Bright Red 314   Evergreen 358

December 1997 to August 1998
Seven paint colours were available:
Arctic Silver metallic 309   Estoril Blue metallic 335
Boston Green metallic 275   Evergreen 358
Bright Red 314   Imola Red II 405
Cosmos Black metallic 303
[Note that Bright Red was only available on European models.]

September 1998 to March 1999
Eight paint colours were available:
Alpine White III 300   Dakar Yellow II 337
Arctic Silver metallic 309   Estoril Blue metallic 335
Boston Green metallic 275   Evergreen 358
Cosmos Black metallic 303   Imola Red II 405

April 1999 to July 2000
There were again eight paint colours:
Alpine White III 300   Evergreen 358
Cosmos Black metallic 303   Imola Red II 405
Dakar Yellow II 337   Oxford Green II metallic 430
Estoril Blue metallic 335   Titanium Silver metallic 354

August 2000 to January 2001
There were just five paint colours:
Alpine White III 300   Oxford Green II metallic 430
Estoril Blue metallic 335   Titanium Silver metallic 354
Imola Red II 405

February 2001 to May 2002
There were nine paint colours:
Alpine White III 300   Oxford Green II metallic 430
Black Sapphire metallic 475   Phoenix Yellow metallic 445
Estoril Blue metallic 335   Steel Grey metallic 400
Imola Red II 405   Titanium Silver metallic 354
Laguna Seca Blue 448

M ROADSTER UPHOLSTERY OPTIONS

Upholstery was in leather as standard, and the choice lay between all-black or black with a contrasting colour.

September 1996 to August 1998
There were five options:
Black Nappa Q6SW
Estoril Blue with Black Nappa Q6ES
Dark Grey with Black Nappa Q6TT
Evergreen with Black Nappa Q6EV
Imola Red with Black Nappa Q6IM

September 1998 to July 2000
There were six options:
Black Nappa Q6SW
Estoril Blue with Black Nappa Q6ES
Dark Grey with Black Nappa Q6TT
Evergreen with Black Nappa Q6EV
Imola Red with Black Nappa Q6IM
Kyalami Orange with Black Nappa Q6KY
[Note that Kyalami Orange with Black Nappa leather was not available on North American CK93 models sold outside the USA.]

February 2001 to May 2002
There were seven options:
Black Nappa Q6SW
Estoril Blue with Black Nappa Q6ES
Dark Beige Nappa with Oregon R3SN
Kiwi with Black Nappa Q6OV
Dark Grey with Black Nappa Q6TT
Laguna Seca Blue + Black Q6LS
Imola Red with Black Nappa Q6IM
[Note that Kiwi with Black Nappa leather was not available on North American (CL93) models.]

■ THE M DIVISION'S Z3

M COUPÉ PAINT OPTIONS

April 1998 to March 1999
Eight paint colours were available:
Alpine White III 300
Arctic Silver metallic 309
Boston Green metallic 275
Cosmos Black metallic 303
Dakar Yellow II 337
Estoril Blue metallic 335
Evergreen 358
Imola Red II 405

April 1999 to June 2000
There were again eight paint colours, this time the same as on the M Roadster:
Alpine White III 300
Cosmos Black metallic 303
Dakar Yellow II 337
Estoril Blue metallic 335
Evergreen 358
Imola Red II 405
Oxford Green II metallic 430
Titanium Silver metallic 354

July 2000 to January 2001
The options were reduced by three to just five paint colours:
Alpine White III 300
Estoril Blue metallic 335
Imola Red II 405
Oxford Green II metallic 430
Titanium Silver metallic 354

February 2001 to May 2002
The same nine paint colours were available as on the M Roadsters:
Alpine White III 300
Black Sapphire metallic 475
Estoril Blue metallic 335
Imola Red II 405
Laguna Seca Blue 448
Oxford Green II metallic 430
Phoenix Yellow metallic 445
Steel Grey metallic 400
Titanium Silver metallic 354

M COUPÉ UPHOLSTERY OPTIONS

As on the M Roadster, upholstery was in leather as standard, and the choice lay between all-black or black with a contrasting colour. The option availability was essentially the same as on M Roadsters, although some options were introduced earlier on the M Coupés.

April 1998 to June 2000
There were seven options:
Black Nappa Q6SW
Evergreen with Black Nappa Q6EV
Dark Beige Nappa with Oregon R3SN I
Imola Red with Black Nappa Q6IM
Dark Grey with Black Nappa Q6TT
Kyalami Orange with Black Nappa Q6KY
Estoril Blue with Black Nappa Q6ES
[Note that Kyalami Orange with Black Nappa leather was not available on North American-specification models sold outside the USA.]

July 2000 to January 2001
The choice was reduced to just four options:
Black Nappa Q6SW
Estoril Blue with Black Nappa Q6ES
Dark Grey with Black Nappa Q6TT
Imola Red with Black Nappa Q6IM

February 2001 to May 2002
There were seven options:
Black Nappa Q6SW
Estoril Blue with Black Nappa Q6ES
Dark Beige Nappa with Oregon R3SN
Kiwi with Black Nappa Q6OV
Dark Grey with Black Nappa Q6TT
Laguna Seca Blue + Black Q6LS
Imola Red with Black Nappa Q6IM
[Note that Kiwi with Black Nappa leather was not available on North American models.]

M ROADSTER PRODUCTION FIGURES

Type	Specification	Production dates	Total
CK91	European, LHD, S50 engine	September 1996 to June 2000	3,557
CK92	European, RHD, S50 engine	November 1997 to June 2000	918
CK93	North American, LHD, S52 engine	February 1998 to July 2000	8,938
CL91	European, LHD, S54 engine	February 2001 to May 2002	271
CL92	European, RHD, S54 engine	February 2001 to April 2002	73
CL93	North American, LHD, S54 engine	February 2001 to May 2002	1,565
		Grand Total	15,322

M COUPÉ PRODUCTION FIGURES

Type	Specification	Production dates	Total
CM91	European, LHD, S50 engine	April 1998 to June 2000	2,178
CM92	European, RHD, S50 engine	August 1998 to June 2000	821
CM93	North American, LHD, S52 engine	July 1998 to June 2000	2,180
CN91	European, LHD, S54 engine	February 2001 to May 2002	269
CN92	European, RHD, S54 engine	February 2001 to May 2002	165
CN93	North American, LHD, S54 engine	February 2001 to May 2002	678
		Grand Total	6,291

VINS AND PRODUCTION DATES

M Roadster

European specification, S50 engine
LB06000–07143	05/97–06/00	1,144	
LD20000–21764	04/96–09/97	1,765	
LD21900–23817	10/97–11/98	1,918	**4,827**

US specification, S52 engine
LC86028–94106	05/98–07/00	8,079	**8,079**
Total, S50- and S52-engined models			**12,906**

European specification, S54 engine
LB64000–64134	04/00–04/02	135	
LJ70000–70383	04/00–05/02	384	**519**

US specification, S54 engine
LJ80000–80921	02/00–09/01	922	**922**
Total, S54-engined models			**1,441**

M Coupé

European specification, S50 engine
LB29000–29460	02/98–03/99	461	
LB55050–57329	09/97–12/97	2,280	**2,741**

US specification, S52 engine
LC60000–62231	10/97–06/00	2,232	**2,232**
Total, S50- and S52-engined models			**4,973**

European specification, S54 engine
LJ90000–90353	04/00–03/02	354	**354**

US specification, S54 engine
LK60000–61339	04/00–05/02	1,340	**1,340**
Total, S54-engined models			**1,694**

(continued overleaf...)

(continued from previous page)

Combined total, all European-specification roadsters
5,346

Combined total, all US-specification roadsters
9,001

Combined total, all M Roadsters 14,347

Combined total, all European-specification coupés
3,095

Combined total, all US-specification coupés
3,572

Combined total, all M Coupés 6,667

Combined total of S50 and S52-engined models
17,879

Combined total of S54-engined models 3,135

GRAND TOTAL, ALL M DERIVATIVES OF THE Z3
21,014

M ROADSTER AND M COUPÉ SPECIFICATIONS

Engines
European models, 1997–2001
Type S50B32 6-cylinder petrol
3201cc (86.4 x 91mm)
Twin ohc, chain-driven
4v per cylinder
Double-VANOS variable valve timing
Seven-bearing crankshaft
Compression ratio 11.3:1
BMW-Siemens MSS 50 engine management system
Three-way catalytic converter standard
321PS (317bhp) at 7,400rpm
350Nm (258lb ft) at 3,250rpm

North American models, 1998–2001
Type S52B32US 6-cylinder petrol
3152cc (86.4 x 89.6mm)
Twin ohc, chain-driven
4v per cylinder
Single-VANOS variable valve timing
Seven-bearing crankshaft
Compression ratio 10.5:1
BMW-Siemens MS41.1 engine management system
Three-way catalytic converter standard
243PS (240bhp) at 6,000rpm
320Nm (236lb ft) at 3,800rpm

All models, 2001–2002
Type S54B32 6-cylinder petrol
3246cc (87 x 89.6mm)
Twin ohc, chain-driven
4v per cylinder
Double-VANOS variable valve timing
Seven-bearing crankshaft
Compression ratio 11.5:1
BMW-Siemens MSS54 engine management system
Three-way catalytic converter standard
325PS (321bhp) at 7,400rpm
350Nm (258lb ft) at 4,900rpm

Transmission
Five-speed ZF Type C manual gearbox
Ratios 4.21:1, 2.49:1, 1.66:1, 1.24:1, 1.00:1

Axle ratio
3.15:1 with S50 and S54 engines
3.23:1 with S52 engine

Suspension, steering and brakes
Front suspension with MacPherson struts, lower L-arms and anti-roll bar
Rear suspension with semi-trailing arms, separate springs and dampers, and anti-roll bar

(continued...)

(continued from previous page)

Rack-and-pinion steering with variable ratio and standard power assistance
Disc brakes all round, twin hydraulic circuits; 315mm (12.4in) ventilated front discs and 312mm (12.28in) ventilated rear discs
ABS standard

Dimensions

Overall length	4,025mm (158.5in)
Overall width	1,740mm (68.5in)
Overall height	1,266mm (49.8in)
Wheelbase	2,459mm (96.8in)
Front track	1,422mm (56.0in)
Rear track	1,493mm (58.8in)

Wheels and tyres

17in five-spoke alloy wheels with 7.5J rims at the front and 9J rims at the rear; 225/45 ZR 17 front tyres and 245/40 ZR 17 rear tyres

Unladen weights

M Roadster (Europe) with S50 engine	1,350kg (2,976lb)
M Roadster (N America) with S52 engine	1,400kg (3,086lb)
M Coupé (Europe) with S50 engine	1,390kg (3,064lb)
M Coupé (N America) with S52 engine	1,420kg (3,131lb)
M Roadster with S54 engine	1,420kg (3,131lb)
M Coupé with S54 engine	1,415kg (3,121lb)

M ROADSTER AND M COUPÉ PERFORMANCE FIGURES

S50 models	0–60mph	5.2sec
	Maximum	155mph (250km/h) (electronically limited)
S52 models	0–60mph	5.5sec
	Maximum	137mph (220km/h)
S54 models	0–60mph	4.7sec
	Maximum	155mph (250km/h) (electronically limited)

CHAPTER FIVE

THE E85 Z4, 2002–2005

It was clear very soon after the introduction of the Z3 in 1995 that BMW had struck a rich seam of customer interest. The immediate success of the Z3 meant that there was no question of this car remaining unique in the BMW line-up: it would have to have a successor. So it was that, by 1998, BMW had begun to focus on what that successor might be.

In the meantime, the 'affordable roadster' market that was the primary target of the Z3 was becoming more crowded. Both MG in Britain (with the MGF) and Alfa Romeo in Italy (with the Spider) had delivered new cars in the same year as when the Z3 had been launched. At a higher price point, Porsche had introduced its Boxster in 1996, and that same year Lotus had introduced its Elise. Mazda's MX-5 arrived in second-generation form in 1997 – and it was well known by 1998 that both Audi (the TT Roadster) and Honda (the S2000) were planning new roadster models for 1999 introduction. All these served to complicate the picture at BMW: how could the new model be made sufficiently distinctive to maintain or improve BMW's share of the market sector?

Certain elements were more or less in place right from the start. If the new model was to be ready to replace the Z3 by the third quarter of 2002, it would need to draw on the mechanical components that BMW expected to have available by then and on the electronic technologies that would be ready for production as well. Of the engines that would be available, the 6-cylinders would have to come from the M54 family that was to make its debut in the 2001-model Z3s. By avoiding a 4-cylinder model – if only in the beginning – BMW could distance themselves from at least some of the competition.

There would, inevitably, be a greater focus on technology: BMW was constantly working on new technology to meet customer demand for it, and this technology was becoming a BMW brand characteristic. The new roadster would not be a proper BMW without such things as the latest generation of traction control and safety systems.

These, though, were the pragmatic building blocks. Just as important was feedback from Z3 customers, whose likes and dislikes had to be fed into the mix. It was clear that the overall proportions of the Z3 were much appreciated: the long-bonnet, short-tail look on a long wheelbase had to be retained. It was too early yet to be certain whether the roadster should be joined by a coupé model, as the Z3 coupé would not reach customers until late 1998. So the main thrust of body design work should focus on the roadster; a coupé could be added to the programme later if sales of the Z3 coupé justified it.

At this stage, the head of BMW design was Chris Bangle, an American who had joined the company in that position in 1992. This was too late for him to have had much influence over the Z3, but his view was that its successor should have a revolutionary rather than evolutionary appearance, and that it should also reflect the family look he was applying to other new BMW designs.

This new look became known as 'flame surfacing' after a motoring journalist tried to describe its characteristics. It was a look that would always be controversial, but it was undeniably distinctive, with the interplay of concave and convex surfaces, hard edges, and smooth, sweeping curves. In practice, Bangle gave the task of lead designer on the new roadster to a Danish-born member of his studio, Anders Warming. Meanwhile, the overall lead on the new project was entrusted to Wolfgang Keelmagen as project director, and chief engineer was Martin Klanner. There was never any doubt that the new car should be built at the Spartanburg plant in the USA, where it would naturally replace the Z3 on the production lines.

An important question, of course, was what to call it. Once again, there seems to have been little doubt about the choice: it should be called the Z4. The name sounded good, and it followed on naturally from the Z3. Customer acceptance was more or less assured.

THE E85 Z4, 2002–2005

The essential lines of the new Z4 roadster are clear from these sketches by Anders Warming, who was responsible for the exterior design. The planned interplay of curved and flat surfaces is already visible at this stage.

Design and Development

From the start, BMW planned to move the Z4 upmarket from the position that the Z3 had occupied. This was partly in pursuit of greater profits, but it was also a strategy that was intended to distance the car from its obvious rivals. So no 4-cylinder engines were planned (and BMW said as much when the car was introduced). Yet, rather bizarrely, the company also claimed at the Z4's launch not to have any plans for an M derivative to replace the M Roadster version of the Z3. Whether that was actually true or was simply a ploy to prevent customers waiting until an M model became available is something that has never been explained.

By the 1990s, it was becoming a motor industry cliché that each new model was bigger than its predecessor. There were of course several reasons for this, not least of which was the need to meet ever-increasing standards of crash safety by providing greater degrees of occupant protection. However, for BMW, making the Z4 physically larger than the Z3 would bring other important benefits. An increase in the wheelbase of 50mm or so (about 2in) would improve the ride quality and would also contribute to greater pas-

■ THE E85 Z4, 2002–2005

This early design sketch, dated 1999, shows ideas for the interior of the Z4. Some would be carried over into production; others, like the twin cowled instrument dials, would not.

Stroke of genius or major mistake? The side repeater indicators were concealed behind a BMW roundel on each front wing – and were one of the first things to be changed when aftermarket tuners got their hands on the Z4.

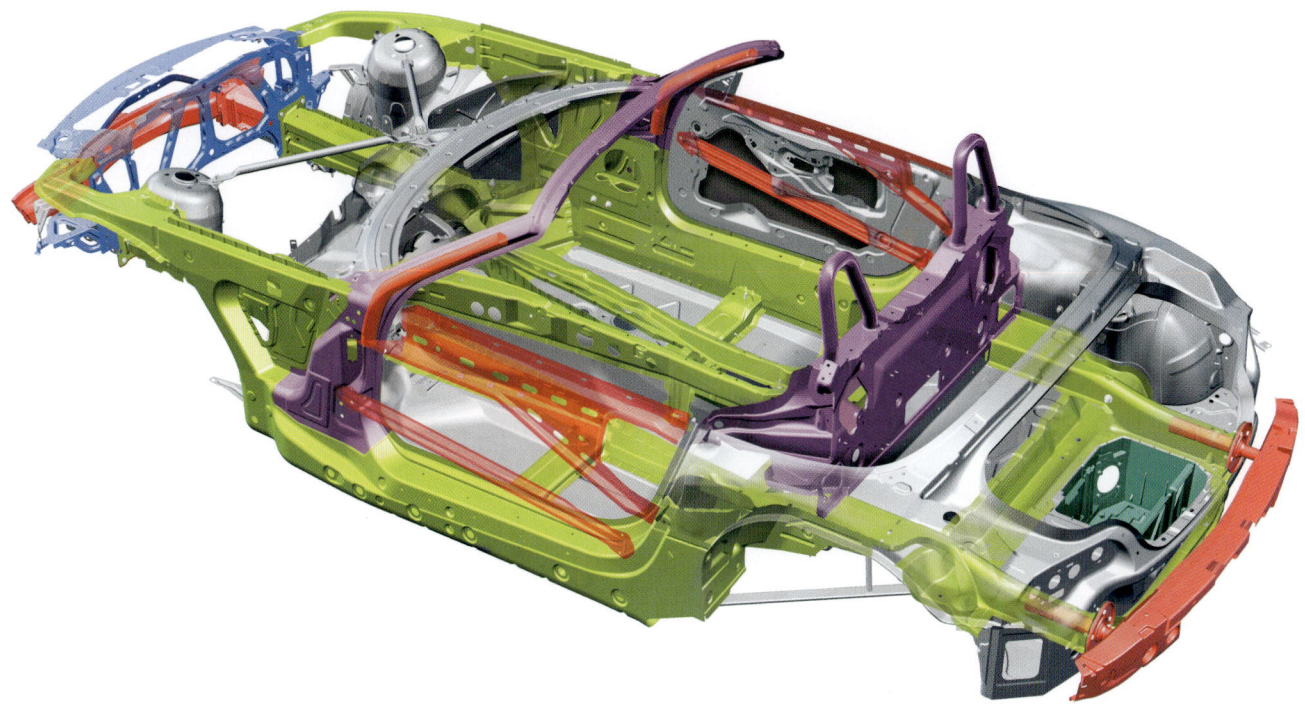

BMW were very proud of the rigidity engineered into the Z4's bodyshell. There was extra strength engineered into the windscreen frame and headrest unit, here highlighted in purple, and the red items were further safety features that protected against rollover accidents and front, rear and side impacts.

senger space without making the car appear unnecessarily large. An increase in width would also provide more room in the passenger cabin and could be used to give the car a more muscular appearance as well. It would also allow for wider tracks that would improve handling and roadholding.

Anders Warming's design made good use of these greater dimensions, incorporating Chris Bangle's overall design principles very skilfully to deliver a shape that both comforted expectations and surprised the onlooker at the same time. The tail had a particularly interesting shape, with a humped boot lid flanked by carefully sculpted lamp units. The roadster bodyshell of the Z4 was also engineered to be stronger in torsion than any other competitive model, and in production form had 14,500Nm (10,695lb ft) per degree of static torsional stiffness. This made it nearly three times as stiff as the bodyshell of the Z3 that it was to replace. Yet there had also been a focus on weight saving, and the car was designed with an aluminium bonnet and magnesium hood supports.

This strong bodyshell made a very obvious contribution to handling precision, but it also earned BMW some excellent results in the EuroNCAP crash tests, where the car achieved four out of a possible five stars. The Z4 would go on to receive a EuroNCAP Best-in-Class award after tests in 2004, when it scored 15.64 points for protection in head-on collisions and 16 points for side impacts, in each case out of a possible maximum result of 16 points. At the time, these were the best figures ever measured on the crash-test dummies in a roadster of any kind.

BMW were also determined to deliver a more sophisticated soft top than the one available on the Z3. A key reason was that the Mercedes-Benz SLK came with a highly acclaimed electric foldaway hardtop as standard (and had done so since 1997). For BMW, a similar device would have introduced unwelcome extra costs and would also have complicated the packaging of the Z4, which was to have a rollover safety system with pop-up bars at the rear. However, the compromise solution was to provide an electrically operated soft top, and with it a proper glass rear window

■ THE E85 Z4, 2002–2005

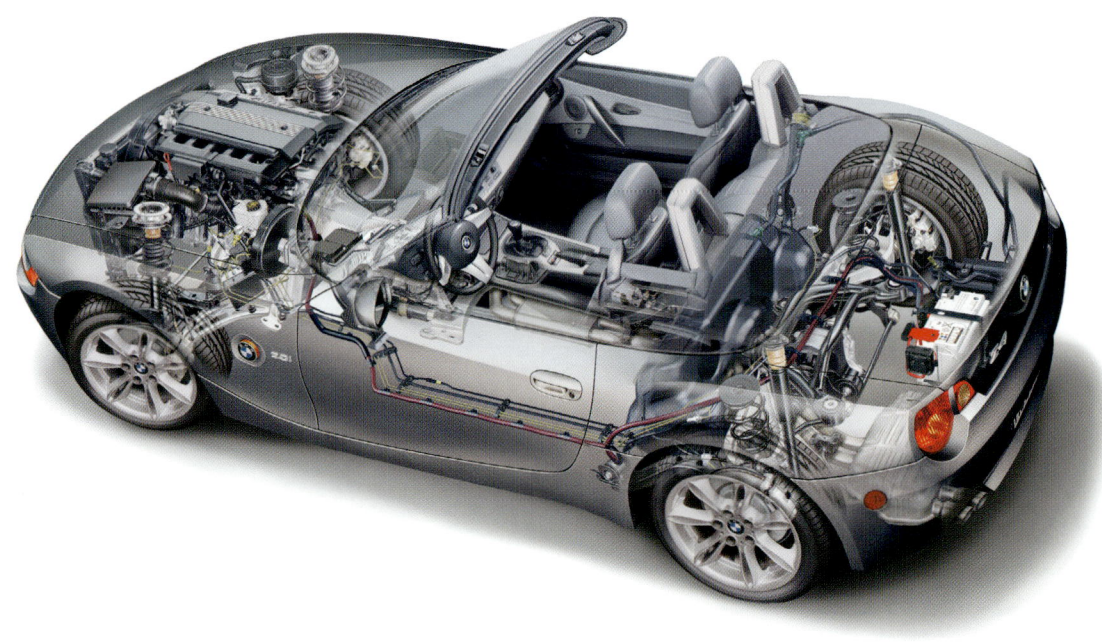

This cutaway drawing was issued when the Z4 was released in 2002, and shows the overall layout of the car, with suspension derived from the E46 3-Series. Note the location of the battery at the rear to improve weight distribution and handling balance.

At the Z4's launch, the engines were 2.5-litre and 3.0-litre derivatives of the M54 6-cylinder. This is almost certainly a 3.0-litre, although there were no obvious visual differences between the two engines. As always with BMWs of the time, the underbonnet scene was neat and almost clinical.

THE E85 Z4, 2002–2005

This early test car was pictured during hot-weather testing. The tape and scribbled lines help to disguise the profile of the car from a distance – but of course do little to hide the lines from close up.

Another early Z4 is seen here on cold-weather test. Once again, the car's lines are disguised with tape, and there are headlamp masks to further confuse the spy photographers who make a living from photographing prototype cars on test. This car also has the optional hardtop in place.

instead of the perspex type that was usually fitted with such roof systems. The system was designed to raise or lower the roof in ten seconds without the need for manually operated clamps on the windscreen header rail. It would be highly acclaimed when the cars went on sale.

For the basic underpinnings, the design team drew on existing production hardware. The suspension was essentially that of the E46 3 Series model, but the Z4 had both a shorter wheelbase and wider tracks. There were different rear track control arms and rear axle carrier bushes, too, to give sharper and more sporting responses than were needed in the E46 saloons and their derivatives. Light alloys kept unsprung weight down, to improve the ride quality.

There would of course be the usual array of electronic traction control aids, including DSC (which could brake individual wheels to restore stability), ASC (which reduced engine power and braked the driven wheels to maintain traction when needed) and Dynamic Traction Control (which acted rather like a limited-slip differential to allow a fast getaway on slippery surface). However, the Z4 project team also wanted to push the envelope further, again at least partly to ensure that the Z4 had some features that

THE E85 Z4, 2002–2005

were not available on rival models. Quite a lot of the BMW appeal came from the marque's use of advanced technology, and two new features chosen for the Z4 typified the need to meet such customer expectations.

The first of these was electric power steering. Its advantages included weight saving as compared to a traditional hydraulic system, but its electric control system also made it easier to 'tune' for greater or lesser sharpness of response. Essentially, sensors and the speedometer delivered information to a central control system that then activated an electric servo motor acting on the steering; in straight-line driving, the sensors detected that there was no torque input into the steering and so the motor supplied no assistance. As soon as the driver turned the wheel, the sensors detected the input and instructed the motor to deliver power assistance appropriate to the car's speed.

The second choice of advanced technology was run-flat tyres, which BMW decided to make standard across the range. The great advantage of these was that the car then needed to carry no spare wheel – not even a space-saver type – so that more space within the body could be devoted to the boot, which could be made more capacious than in the typical traditional two-seat roadster. So the Z4 ended up with 240ltr (8.5cu ft) of boot space as well as a decently sized 55ltr (12gal) fuel tank, the latter being a big improvement over the tiny tank that had been adversely criticized on the Z3 models.

The First Z4s

Volume production of the new Z4 Roadster began at Spartanburg on 1 September 2002. The car was introduced to the world at the Paris Motor Show later that month. The US showroom launch was on 22 October, and the first customers took delivery of their new cars during November. British buyers had to contain their patience for another eight months; sales of right-hand-drive Z4s began there in June 2003. Prices worldwide were around 10 per cent higher than those of equivalent Z3 models.

The model range was straightforward and simple. The entry-level model was the 2.5i, with its 194PS (192bhp),

The real thing: the swoops and curves catch the light in this view of a 2003-model car. The round red lights in the bumper apron are US-market side marker lights, and the car is a 3.0i model, wearing attractive optional five-spoke alloy wheels.

THE E85 Z4, 2002–2005

This is the interior of a **Z4** with the standard specification, featuring fabric upholstery. The arrangement of the air vents and controls in the centre of the dash was particularly neat.

The seats in this car are upholstered in leather, and the dashboard has the high-line navigation system with its foldaway screen. The rather plain-looking dashboard on the passenger's side conceals an **SRS** airbag.

■ THE E85 Z4, 2002–2005

The instrument binnacle was designed to look sporty but, more importantly, to convey its information easily to the driver. These are the instruments on a left-hand-drive model with 260km/h speedometer.

This was the selector lever of the automatic models, and this left-hand drive car is fitted with the 'Sport' button that called the Dynamic Drive Control system into play.

There were elements of both theatre and sculpture about the door panels with their sweeping handles and armrests. The electric window switch is integrated into the armrest, and the main door panel carries an ICE speaker.

2.5-litre M54 engine, while its more expensive alternative was the 3.0i with a longer-stroke M54 engine that delivered 233PS (230bhp). The 2.5i could hit 146mph (235km/h) while the 3.0i was limited to a 155mph (250km/h) top speed. Both models came with manual gearboxes as standard, a five-speed in the 2.5i and a six-speed in the 3.0i. The alternative Steptronic automatic gearbox cost extra in both cases, and both could also be ordered with a six-speed SMG clutchless manual gearbox.

That was just the start of the options list. Standard upholstery was Sensatec Free Spirit cloth (not the snappiest of names), but there was a leather option, and the cockpit trim was available in brushed aluminium or polished wood. There were two different satellite navigation systems, one providing its guidance on the radio display panel and the more expensive alternative using a foldaway screen in the centre of the dash top. The satnav systems depended on DVD rather than the less capacious CD discs for the first time on a BMW. Then, of course, there were alloy wheel options, including two 18in sizes. Cars could be ordered with Xenon headlights, a cruise control and a variety of audio system upgrades.

There were seven paint colours at launch, some of them carried over from the Z3 range. However, the range was increased from April 2003 as production built up to its anticipated volume, and three new paints (Alpine White, Bright Red and Toledo Blue) lightened up the colour palette.

The 2004 Models

As the Z4 range settled into its stride, BMW broadened the engine options for the 2004 season with the introduction of a new entry-level model. This was a 2.2-litre car, announced in October 2003 but not available immediately in all Z4 markets. There were some minor changes, too, and perhaps the most significant of those was the introduction of a button on the transmission tunnel by the gear lever that transformed the car's behaviour. The Sport button sharpened the engine's response to the accelerator and also reduced the amount of assistance from the electric power steering to give the car a more sporting feel. Formally known as Dynamic Drive Control, this system had also been seen on the current M3 and M5 models and had been previewed at the Z4's launch in 2002.

Clearly, customer feedback had demanded this greater focus on sporting characteristics, because a new Sport package also became available at extra cost. Central to this was a stiffened and lowered suspension, but it was accompanied by larger wheels as well. For the 2.5i models, there were 17in wheels in place of the 16in size now standard, while the 3.0i (now on 17in wheels as standard) took on 18in wheels with 225/40 tyres at the front and 255/35 tyres at the rear.

Meanwhile, both 2.5i and 3.0i types became available with Xenon headlamps at extra cost, and leather upholstery was made standard on the bigger-engined car, although it remained an extra-cost option for the 2.5i. BMW dealers were now able to install a wind deflector (as before, a net deployed behind the seats) and a removable hardtop.

These changes perhaps marked the beginning of BMW's recognition that the Z4 had not been quite as much of a hit as the company had hoped. Although there certainly were markets where it was much liked – Britain being one of them – it had not gone down very well in either Germany or the USA. As these were expected to be major markets for the car, something had to be done.

One reason for these disappointing sales was undoubtedly the stiffer competition in the marketplace. Both the Porsche Boxster and the Audi TT were presenting serious competition for the Z4, and the second-generation Mercedes-Benz SLK was due to reach the market in 2004. So it must have been around 2004 that BMW began to think in terms of broadening the Z4 range to a greater extent than they had originally planned. In the meantime, however, the new 2.2i model extended it downwards. This had the 172PS (168bhp) 2.2-litre version of the M54 6-cylinder engine and was badged as a 2.2i.

The Z4 2.2i was most easily recognizable by the bright metal 2.2i badge on each front wing, but it also had different grille slats and headlamp surrounds from the 2.5i and 3.0i models. Standard wear were 16in alloy wheels, although there was the usual array of extra-cost alternatives, and the model came with the standard rapid electric soft-top deployment and rollbar protection systems. Deletions from the accepted Z4 specification were minimal, although the 2.2i had a manual air conditioning system rather than the fully automatic type and came with a five-speed manual gearbox or an automatic at extra cost. It also had Free Spirit Sensatec technical fabric upholstery – cloth rather than leather, in other words.

There were sacrifices in performance, of course, but the 2.2i model's 7.7sec 0–60mph time (8.3sec with automatic) was no disgrace and, as *BMW Car* magazine put it after testing one for its February 2004 issue, the short-stroke engine 'was the sweetest and most willing BMW unit we've had the pleasure of sitting behind for a long time'.

Even though sales of the Z4 had been disappointing in some markets, the car was most definitely selling strongly. Over its six-and-a-half-year lifetime, the Z3 had sold an average of just over 43,000 cars per year. Yet the Z4 was doing far better: just two years after Z4 production had begun, the 100,000th example was completed at Spartanburg as evidence that annual production of the newer model was around 50,000. For the record, that car was shipped to Jena, near Leipzig in Germany, and was finished with a BMW Individual colour of Phoenix Yellow. It also had 18in alloy wheels and leather upholstery in Phoenix Yellow and Anthracite with silver aluminium cabin trim.

What the Press Thought

Right from the start, three things about the Z4 provoked negative criticism – and that must have been rather a shock to BMW. One was the styling which, to be fair, always polarized opinions. Some people loathed it and others loved it; during the preparation stages of this book, one lady remembered thinking that the car looked like a squashed shoe when she first saw one, while another (younger) one eulogized about it as unbelievably sexy.

Another feature that attracted negative comment was the electric power steering, which many people thought had sacrificed feel (and driver appeal) on the altar of technology. And the third was the run-flat tyres, which simply did not offer the ride and handling qualities available from more conventional types. So two of the advanced technological features that had been intended to give the car additional appeal actually seemed to be having the effect of lessening its appeal. All these criticisms showed up early on in the reports published in the press.

The press ride-and-drive launch was held in the Algarve region of Portugal, but only 3.0i models were available and all were American-specification cars. *Autocar* editor Steve Sutcliffe was more than a little negative about the car's sporting qualities when he tried one and the story he wrote, complaining of serious understeer, 'caused serious disquiet at BMW HQ' according to the magazine's 25 June 2003 issue. In that issue, *Autocar* reported on the UK press launch, held

THE E85 Z4, 2002–2005

Every inch a sports roadster – or at least that is how the Z4 looks in this shot of a 2003 model issued to the media when the car was launched.

The rear view was unmistakable, thanks to the humped boot lid and the carefully sculpted tail lights. The rollover bars behind the seats were finished in silver, regardless of the body colour.

around Aberdeen in Scotland with UK-spec cars, and this time Colin Goodwin reported rather more favourably. Even so, he could see problems with the styling: 'I rather like the look of the thing, though I'm equally certain it'll date faster than one of Beckham's Man Utd shirts.'

The steering, with the sharper suspension settings used on UK cars, was still 'not perfect. It does its job in saving energy right enough, but the feel is rather artificial and not as good as a really well sorted, hydraulically assisted rack-and-pinion system.'

A different team of *Autocar* testers assessed a 2.5i model for that magazine's 16 July 2003 issue. 'It would still be possible to grumble that the Z4 hasn't put right all that was wrong with its predecessor,' they summarized. 'Although dynamically superior to the Z3 in every respect it's still not quite as involving as some of us would like.' However, this team of testers described the electric power steering system as 'one of the best we've tried'; found the 2.5-litre engine 'incredibly refined'; and thought that the Z4 2.5i was 'a grown-up rag-top, a paragon of refinement with a beautiful interior and a clever roof'. And, they added, 'it's also quick enough to make you wonder whether it's worth shelling out for the bigger 3.0-litre engine.'

Meanwhile, one-marque magazine *BMW Car* had been highly impressed by its first acquaintance with the Z4 3.0i in Portugal. Editor Bob Harper wrote in the December 2002 issue:

> Bury the throttle in any of the six gears and you'll be rewarded with rapid forward momentum as the stubby rear squats down and the long bonnet rises as you rapidly haul in the horizon. It's a hugely flexible piece of kit thanks to its bi-Vanos variable valve timing but there's still plenty left to entertain at the engine's top end.

Harper also liked the fact that there was more room in the cockpit than in the rather cramped Z3, but he did not like the polished wood trim option, which 'just looked completely out of keeping with the rest of the cars' high-tech, modern feel'. He also felt that the 3.0i would prove a very strong rival for the Porsche Boxster, the car by which others in the two-seat roadster sector were then judged. 'Where the Z4 scores over the Boxster is in its all-round ability; its blend of magic carpet ride, handling and roadholding gives it the edge. . . . The Z4 [also] wins on price.'

In the USA, when one-marque magazine *Bimmer* reported on the 2004-model Z4s in its issue dated February 2004, its disappointment was palpable. Of the several examples its staff had driven since the car's launch in 2002, 'none have really met our expectations of a good European sports car . . . the Z4 just isn't focused enough to succeed.' They were unimpressed with the latest extra-cost Extended Leather option because 'there are already several grades, textures and colors of plastic and leather on various surfaces, so there just doesn't seem to be any reason to introduce yet another'. They also noted that all Z4s had 'uncomfortable and under-bolstered chairs', and 'we found the navigation function to be disappointingly slow to program and operate', adding that they would stick to an old-fashioned road atlas and a compass until BMW had improved the system.

Although the 3.0-litre M54 engine was 'enchanting', they had reservations about the steering, which was 'quick but over-boosted and uncommunicative', and they found that the car 'never feels totally composed or sure-footed, especially over anything but glass-smooth surfaces'. The real vitriol, however, was reserved for the SMG gearbox fitted to the test car. The magazine suggested its initials might stand for Slower-than-Manual-Gearbox. 'Downshifts are quick and generally smooth, but upshifts are slow to the point of annoyance.'

Shifts were quicker and slicker in Sport mode, which raised the question of why the non-Sport mode existed at all. As fitted to the Z4, the SMG was nowhere near as good as its equivalent on the M3: *Bimmer* complained of

> the lurching and jerking in the lower gears, the irritating pause each time first gear or reverse is selected and the infuriating delay that occurs while the transmission is debating whether it wants to downshift to first or stay in second at very low speeds.

More generally,

> the system is lazy, sluggish and not nearly aggressive enough to offer any real benefit over a good manual. Considering that we find just the opposite to be true of the M3's SMG gearbox, we remain unconvinced that BMW has a clear understanding of what role the Z4 is intended to fill.

THE E85 Z4, 2002–2005

AFTERMARKET TUNERS

Whether BMW's claims at launch that it had no plans for an M derivative of the Z4 was true or simply intended to deflect interest in higher-performance models is still open to question. However, it did have the effect of opening the floodgates to a variety of aftermarket Z4 performance conversions. Over the next two years, there were cars from AC Schnitzer, Alpina, Hamann Motorsport, Hartge, Infinitas and Rennsport. All of these were built in relatively small numbers, not least because of their high prices, and as all were essentially bespoke conversions it is likely that no two cars were exactly the same.

AC Schnitzer

AC Schnitzer were very quick off the mark with their offering, which was announced at the Geneva Motor Show in March 2003 and went on sale that autumn. Central to this one was Schnitzer's existing C30 engine, a supercharged version of the M54 3.0-litre that delivered 295bhp at 6,300rpm and 400Nm (295lb ft) of torque at 4,800rpm. This delivered 0–100km/h (0–62mph) acceleration in around 5.3sec with a maximum speed of around 170mph (274km/h).

The Schnitzer car was also lowered by about 25mm and ran on 19in Star-spoke alloy wheels with 8.5in front rims and 9in rear rims, wearing 235/35 and 265/30 tyres respectively. A strut brace between the suspension top mounts stiffened the front end, and there were uprated brakes. Cosmetic changes included a deeper front spoiler and rear apron, cooling ducts in the side skirts and a winglet spoiler on each side of the humped boot lid. The roundel indicator units in the wings were replaced by a strange slatted highlight feature in chrome, incorporating a small side repeater, plus an AC Schnitzer logo. The cabin had carbon fibre trim, alloy pedals and handbrake grip, and Schnitzer logos on the leather seats.

Alpina

Well-established BMW specialist Alpina took its time before delivering an uprated Z4 but had its Alpina Roadster S model ready in the first quarter of 2004. The car came with the 3.4-litre engine that Alpina was already

(*continued overleaf...*)

Alpina's Roadster S had a 3.4-litre engine, strikingly attractive alloy wheels and other visual changes from the original. This one was the right-hand-drive demonstrator used by Sytner, the UK Alpina importers.

THE E85 Z4, 2002–2005

(continued from previous page)

using in its B3S model, with 3346cc, 300bhp at 6,300rpm and 266lb ft of torque at 4,800rpm. Performance claims were 0–60mph in 5.1sec and a maximum speed of 169mph (272km/h), or 172mph (277km/h) if the car was fitted with the optional hardtop. Alpina retained the six-speed manual gearbox, somewhat reworked, even though its BMW-based models in recent years had often used automatic gearboxes.

The Alpina rear spoiler was notable for running the full width of the boot lid, across the characteristic centre hump, and the Roadster S came with Alpina's supremely attractive 19in Dynamic wheels (with five sets of four spokes), with 8.5in front rims and 9.5in rear rims. The tyres were conventional types rather than the run-flats on the standard car. All cars had a 3.4S badge on each front wing, and there was an extra-cost Lux model with additional items such as Xenon headlamps, cruise control, satellite navigation, a CD multi-changer and an Alpina-branded wind deflector.

Hamann

Hamann Motorsport's HM3.3 conversion was available by autumn 2003 and, as its name suggests, came with a 3.3-litre engine. This delivered 286bhp at 6,200rpm and 262lb ft at 4,000rpm, and Hamann claimed a 0–100km/h (0–62mph) time of 5.0sec with a maximum speed of 168mph (270km/h). The engine was bored out to 86mm and had a special crankshaft to give a 93.8mm stroke. The cylinder head was machined and the engine had sports camshafts and high-performance valve springs. Also available were an induction kit, plus a special exhaust manifold with a metal-bed sports catalyst and a four-pipe exhaust.

The Hamann car came with lowered suspension and multi-piece 19in wheels; the brakes were ventilated and slotted discs with four-pot calipers at the front and a larger than standard diameter. An 'aerokit' of front spoiler and side skirts could be had, with a two-piece boot-lid wing spoiler. There were two types of rear diffuser to suit either twin or quad tailpipes, and an air intake moulding replaced the BMW roundel on each front wing.

Hartge

Hartge prepared two different versions of the Z4, one powered by a 5.0-litre V8 engine and the other by a supercharged version of the 3.0-litre straight-six engine. Like Alpina, Hartge had manufacturer status in Germany, so its Z4 models carried full Hartge identification and Hartge's own VINs.

The V8 car was ready by summer 2003 and was a massively expensive machine that used several components from BMW's E39 M5 saloon. The V8 engine (400bhp at 6,600rpm and 369lb ft at 3,800rpm) was accompanied by the M5's six-speed gearbox with a short-throw shift, and the Sport button of the standard Z4 was deleted as redundant. The 0–100km/h (0–62mph) time was claimed to be 4.6sec and the maximum speed 187mph (301km/h). There was a fully adjustable coilover suspension and the 19in wheels were accompanied by special eight-pot front brakes with 380mm drilled discs and by the 325mm drilled rear discs with four-pot calipers from the E46 M3. A limited-slip M Differential was also fitted.

On the cosmetic side, the 5.0-litre Hartge car had a redesigned front apron with the company's trademark split air intake, and a centre-exit exhaust with a '5.0' badge on the tail. The side repeaters were replaced by Hartge roundels and repeaters with clear lenses.

Hartge's 6-cylinder Z4 became available about a year after the V8 model. Considerably less expensive, it had the company's supercharged version of the 3.0-litre M54 engine, as seen in their 330i models, although with the supercharger itself relocated to suit space within the Z4's engine bay. This engine delivered 310bhp and 295lb ft of torque to give 0–100km/h (0–62mph) in 5.3sec and a top speed of around 170mph (274km/h). Hartge's 19in multi-spoke wheels were available, with an adjustable sports suspension that lowered the car by about 25mm. On the inside, cosmetic changes were accompanied by a short-throw gear change.

Infinitas

Infinitas was a new German tuning company, with headquarters at Aresing, and chose the Z4 as the subject of its first conversion. This was ready by the start of 2004.

(continued opposite...)

THE E85 Z4, 2002–2005

Special multi-spoke alloy wheels and lower body addenda distinguish this Z4 from Infinitas, whose work centred on a supercharged engine.

(*continued from previous page*)

Like other tuners, Infinitas supercharged the 3.0-litre engine, using an ASA supercharger with 0.35–0.45 bar of boost to achieve 320bhp at 5,900rpm and 310lb ft at 2,800rpm. Claimed performance was 5.2sec for 0–60mph and a maximum speed of 168mph (270km/h). On automatic models, power was limited to 300bhp, but the company also planned a 360bhp version of the engine for later.

The Infinitas Z4 was lowered by 20mm (0.79in) and had 19in alloy wheels with uprated springs and anti-roll bars and an aluminium tie bar between the front suspension towers. Larger brake discs and calipers came from the BMW parts bin. This conversion was more about performance than looks, but the interior was also changed with Alcantara in place of the standard aluminium or wood trim items.

Rennsport

US tuning specialists Rennsport were based in Los Angeles and drew up their Z4SR conversion to suit the rather different requirements of the US market. Here, restrictive nationwide speed limits inevitably put more focus on acceleration than on top speed, which was far more important in Germany with its derestricted Autobahns. The Z4SR became available over the summer of 2004.

Rennsport followed the popular supercharging route to getting more power from the Z4's 3.0-litre engine, and used an intercooled ASA SK1 supercharger with a special exhaust system to achieve 360bhp and 320lb ft. In pursuit of maximum acceleration, they fitted a lower 3.46:1 final drive with a torsen differential – the result was a 0–60mph time of 4.6sec.

Rennsport fitted adjustable coilover suspension all round, lowering the ride height by a full 60mm – which would have been too much for European roads. They added uprated anti-roll bars and Brembo four-piston brakes with 19in BBS alloy wheels. The first car also had a custom-made body kit of wider aluminium wheel arches front and rear allied to elements drawn from BMW's own M-Tech body kit.

THE E85 Z4, 2002–2005

That was strong criticism, and so was this summary:

> Extra leather and electronic gadgets might please the boulevardier, but what this car really needs is a complete reworking of the chassis, a decent pair of seats and a sequential gearbox that's every bit as willing and able as the engine it is mated to.

And yet... on its introduction in 2002, the Z4 had won *Automobile Magazine*'s 'Design of the Year Award' in the USA. Clearly, this was going to be a controversial model for BMW.

The 2005 and 2006 Model Years

The 2005-model Z4s were very much a continuation of what had gone before. Nevertheless, some welcome new options came with them in autumn 2004, such as heated seats and a navigation system, plus the BMW Assist emergency and concierge service. Take-up of the SMG gearbox on the 2.5i models had clearly been small, because the option was dropped for those cars although it remained available for the 3.0i.

Meanwhile, back at BMW headquarters in Munich, the company's engineers were working on three developments that had been expressly ruled out when the cars were launched in 2002. In response to media questions, they had said that there would be no 4-cylinder model, that there would be no coupé derivative, and that there would be no Z4 derivatives from the M division. By mid-2006, all three answers had been proved inaccurate.

The truth was probably that all three models were in the plan but that they had not yet been signed off for production – so the responses to the media were true at the time they were spoken, even if they were deliberately misleading as well. Less clear is whether the autumn 2005 arrival of a 4-cylinder car and the coincident 'tease' of a concept coupé (see Chapter 6) were events that had been brought forward in the schedule to help tackle slower Z4 sales than BMW had expected.

One way or the other, the 4-cylinder car was introduced in October 2005 as the Z4 2.0i, and was very clearly intended to bring the entry-level price of the range down in the hope of picking up additional sales volume. The car came without the much-liked electrically operated soft top, which helped keep its price down, and of course its 4-cylinder engine drove manufacturing costs down still further.

Yet the 2.0i was still a proper Z4, and its 137mph (220km/h) top speed was just 3mph (5km/h) below the maximum of the 6-cylinder 2.2i that had been the previous entry-level model. Acceleration was slower, of course, and the 0–100km/h (0–62mph) sprint took 8.2sec as against 7.7sec in the 2.2i. Overall fuel consumption was around 5mpg better, and these factors together with attractive pricing certainly put pressure on the 6-cylinder model. Its demise was not long in coming: it lasted only until the end of the 2006 model year.

The 2.0i had particular interest in that its 150PS (148bhp) 4-cylinder engine was from the new N46 family, introduced in 2004 and built at BMW's Hams Hall factory in the UK. These engines had aluminium cylinder blocks and twin ohc with Double-VANOS operating 4v per cylinder; they also featured new Valvetronic and DISA technology (which is explained in the next chapter). From the outside, onlookers would be hard pressed to distinguish a 2.0i model from its 6-cylinder siblings, especially if the tail badge had been removed and optional larger alloys had been fitted; the only real giveaway was the single tailpipe instead of the twin pipes of the 6-cylinder cars.

The October 2005 Frankfurt Motor Show also provided the first hint that BMW's earlier denial of plans for a coupé derivative of the Z4 may have been misleading. For there on the manufacturer's stand was a metallic silver Z4 concept coupé. Few people who saw that can have doubted that it would enter production as the long-awaited replacement for the Z3 Coupé – and that was precisely BMW's intention. The new coupé would not be introduced for several more months, but the concept model allowed BMW to build customer anticipation and to gather valuable extra publicity for the Z4 range. When the Z4 Coupé eventually did appear, it would be identical to the concept car, give or take the rather fussy design of alloy wheels and the show-car interior displayed on the concept model.

THE E85 Z4, 2002–2005

ABOVE AND BELOW: **Like the Z3 before it, the Z4 was built at BMW's Spartanburg plant in South Carolina. As before, overhead conveyors were used, and presented the part-assembled cars to line workers at a convenient height.**

Z4 PAINT OPTIONS, 2003–2005 MODELS

The paints listed here are the standard showroom colours. It was of course possible to order colours from the BMW Individual custom-finishing catalogue at extra cost.

2003 model year

Colour/BMW code	Colour/BMW code
Alpine White 300	Silver A08
Black Sapphire metallic 475	Sterling Grey met 472
Bright Red 314	Titanium Silver metallic 354
Jet Black 668	Toledo Blue metallic 482
Maldives Blue metallic A15	Urban Green A04
Merlot Red A02	

Alpine White, Bright Red and Toledo Blue were not available until April 2003.

2004–2005 model years

Colour/BMW code	Colour/BMW code
Alpine White 300	Olivine Green 349
Black Sapphire metallic 475	Sterling Grey metallic 472
Bright Red 314	Titanium Silver 354
Jet Black 668	Toledo Blue metallic 482
Maldives Blue metallic A15	Urban Green A04
Merlot Red A02	

Olivine Green was introduced in April 2004 to replace Urban Green.

Z4 SPECIFICATIONS, 2003–2005 MODELS

Engines

2.0-litre
Type N46B20 4-cylinder petrol
1995cc (84 × 90mm)
Twin ohc, chain-driven
4v per cylinder
Double-VANOS variable valve timing, Valvetronic control and DISA variable inlet manifold
Five-bearing crankshaft
Compression ratio 10.5:1
Bosch engine management system
Three-way catalytic converter standard
150PS (148bhp) at 6,200rpm
200Nm (148lb ft) at 3,600rpm

2.2-litre
Type M54B22 6-cylinder petrol
2171cc (80 × 72mm)
Twin ohc, chain-driven
4v per cylinder
Double-VANOS variable valve timing
Seven-bearing crankshaft
Compression ratio 10.8:1
Siemens engine management system
Three-way catalytic converter standard
170PS (168bhp) at 6,100rpm
210Nm (150lb ft) at 3,500rpm

2.5-litre
Type M54B25 6-cylinder petrol
2494cc (84 × 75mm)
Twin ohc, chain-driven
4v per cylinder
Double-VANOS variable valve timing
Seven-bearing crankshaft
Compression ratio 10.5:1
Siemens engine management system
Three-way catalytic converter standard
194PS (192bhp) at 6,000rpm
237Nm (175lb ft) at 3,500rpm

3.0-litre
Type M54B30 6-cylinder petrol
2979cc (84 × 89.6mm)
Twin ohc, chain-driven
4v per cylinder
Double-VANOS variable valve timing
Seven-bearing crankshaft
Compression ratio 10.2:1
Siemens MS45 engine management system giving sequential fuel injection
Three-way catalytic converter standard
233PS (230bhp) at 5,900rpm
300Nm (222lb ft) at 3,500rpm

Transmission
Five-speed ZF manual gearbox standard (2.5i)
    Ratios 4.23:1, 2.52:1, 1.66:1, 1.22:1, 1.00:1
Six-speed Getrag manual gearbox standard (3.0i)
    Ratios 4.35:1, 2.50:1, 1.66:1, 1.24:1, 1.00:1, 0.85:1
Six-speed SMG sequential gearbox optional

Axle ratio
3.23:1   (2.5i manual)
3.93:1   (3.0i manual)

Suspension, steering and brakes
Front suspension with MacPherson struts, double wishbones, coil springs and anti-roll bar
Rear suspension with multiple links, coil springs and anti-roll bar
Rack-and-pinion steering with 14.2:1 ratio and standard electric power assistance
Disc brakes all round, with twin hydraulic circuits; ABS standard; 2.5i with 286mm ventilated front discs and 280mm ventilated rear discs; 3.0i with 300mm ventilated front discs and 294mm ventilated rear discs

(continued opposite...)

(continued from opposite page)

Dimensions

Overall length	4,090mm (161.0in)
Overall width	1,780mm (70.1in); 1,904mm (74.9in) over mirrors
Overall height	1,300mm (51.2in)
Wheelbase	2,495mm (98.2in)
Front track	1,473mm (58in)
Rear track	1,523mm (60in)

Wheels and tyres

2.5i	7J x 16 alloy wheels with 225/50 R 16 run-flat tyres
4.0i	8J x 17 alloy wheels with 225/45 ZR 17 run-flat tyres

Unladen weights

2.0i manual	1,225kg (2,700lb)
2.5i manual	1,260kg (2,778lb)
3.0i manual	1,290kg (2,844lb)

Z4 PERFORMANCE FIGURES, 2003–2005 MODELS

2.0i Roadster	0–100km/h (0–62mph)	8.2sec
	Maximum	137mph (220km/h)
2.2i	0–60mph	7.7sec
	Maximum	140mph (225km/h)
2.5i	0–60mph	7.0sec
	Maximum	146mph (235km/h)
3.0i	0–60mph	5.9sec
	Maximum	155mph (250km/h) (governed)

CHAPTER SIX

MAKEOVER – THE 2006–2008 MODELS

BMW had planned from the start to give the Z4 range its midlife overhaul in 2006, and the outline of the revised model range had been drawn up when Wolfgang Keelmagen was still running the project. He had handed over to Martin Klanner, who had been chief engineer during the original car's development, and although the basic plan remained in place, it was adjusted to take account of developments that were outside BMW's control.

Market conditions had changed slightly since the original plan had been formulated. In particular, it became clear that Porsche now planned to introduce its revised Boxster for the 2006 model year. Although BMW had anticipated revisions to this key Z4 rival, they had not been able to pin down exactly when it would reach the showrooms. Once they knew a date, they could adjust their plans to suit, and in practice they decided to hold back the introduction of the revised Z4s until April 2006. That would avoid the two cars reaching the market together, which could have been harmful to sales on both sides, and it would allow BMW a few months to tweak their Z4 if the features of the Porsche presented a particular challenge.

The Z4 Concept Coupé was shown in the autumn of 2005, but there would be no production coupés before the facelifted Z4 models arrived during 2006. The concept car was of course fully drivable, and was very close to the way the production models would be. Note, though, the absence of marker lights from the front wing, which would be a feature of the production cars.

MAKEOVER – THE 2006–2008 MODELS

ABOVE: The coupé bodyshell was even stiffer than that of the roadster, and this view of the Concept Coupé with its big hatchback open gives some idea of why: the roof pillars and roof itself look very solid. Note the rear lights, which differ from the early roadster type but are not the same as those of the later facelifted cars.

RIGHT: The complex spoked design of the Concept Coupé's alloy wheels was either attractive or fussy, depending on your viewpoint – it did not enter production.

■ MAKEOVER – THE 2006–2008 MODELS

The interior of the Concept Coupé was certainly an attention-grabber, but was not what BMW intended for production.

This photograph of the Concept Coupé head-to-head with a 2005 Roadster shows how the fixed-roof car retained all the basic lines of the open model. The two had been designed together, even though the announcement of the coupé was delayed.

MAKEOVER – THE 2006–2008 MODELS

The rear view of the Concept Coupé was resolved right from the start, resulting in an infinitely better looking car than its Z3 equivalent.

Although the revised cars are sometimes described as 2006 models, they arrived so late in the season that to all intents and purposes they were early 2007 models. In Britain, deliveries did not in fact start until August 2006, which was more or less the traditional start of the new season. There were then relatively few changes to the Z4 after the midlife makeover.

However, that makeover brought changes in three main areas. First, the Z4's appearance was freshened by a cosmetic facelift both inside and outside; second, the roadster body was joined by a coupé derivative; and third, a clutch of new engines both broadened the appeal of the range and enhanced existing models. Of the engines in the revised Z4s, only the 4-cylinder 2-litre introduced for the 2005 model year was carried over. The rest were all new – including a high-performance type from the M division that is discussed in more detail in Chapter 7.

The realigned Z4 line-up also showed some clear distinctions between the European (ECE) and US ranges, notably in the choice of engines available. There were five different Roadsters for ECE markets, badged as 2.0i, 2.5i, 2.5si, 3.0si and Z4 M, plus two different Coupés, badged as 3.0si and Z4 M. The USA, however, had just three Roadsters (3.0i, 3.0si and Z4 M) plus the two Coupés (3.0si and Z4 M).

MAKEOVER – THE 2006–2008 MODELS

CHANGES AT SPARTANBURG

The assembly line for BMW two-seat Z models at Spartanburg was joined by an assembly line for the X5 Sports Activity Vehicle in 1999. These two lines ran separately until the end of 2005.

The entire plant was subsequently reconfigured so that a single assembly line was capable of building both Z4s and X5s, and all volume-production 'facelift' Z4s were built on the new assembly line. The new system was designed to give maximum production flexibility, and eventually to allow other models to go down the same assembly line as well. BMW claimed at the time that the Spartanburg assembly plant would in future be able to build anything from 100 per cent X5s to a 60:40 split between Z4s and X5s.

Within two years, Spartanburg would go on to become the global centre of SUV assembly for BMW, while the second-generation Z4 would be built in Germany from 2008.

The Powertrains

As that list of model designations above shows, the 2.2i model disappeared from the range, leaving the 4-cylinder 2.0i as the entry-level model. The 6-cylinder 'mainstream' engines were 2.5-litre and 3.0-litre types, as they had been before, but both belonged to the new N52 family of lightweight engines.

All of the new Z4 engines had previously been used in other BMW models, especially the E90 3 Series cars, but all were still relatively new. Like the 4-cylinder 2-litre, the new 6-cylinder engines depended on electronic control systems which were more easily reconfigured than earlier types, a factor that allowed BMW to provide versions of the same engine in different states of tune with minimum additional manufacturing cost.

In addition to the VANOS variable camshaft timing technology that had been seen on the earlier M54 engines, the new engines also benefited from both Valvetronic and DISA. The two systems worked with VANOS (again applied to both camshafts) to give very precise control of engine behaviour so that optimum engine response was available at all speeds and under all load conditions.

DISA was a variable-length inlet tract system, while Valvetronic controlled the amount of inlet valve lift. It actually worked through an electric stepper motor which adjusted the position of the finger followers and rockers that opened the valves. With Valvetronic, there was no need for a throttle plate to control the amount of air entering the cylinders, and this reduced pumping losses while improving efficiency by up to 10 per cent at part-throttle openings and speeding up engine response. Without a throttle plate, however, there was no vacuum created in the inlet manifold, so the Valvetronic engines had to have a separate vacuum generator to provide vacuum for the brake servo and emissions control systems.

The two new 6-cylinder engines were both members of BMW's latest N52 family, originally introduced in 2004 at the same time as the N46 4-cylinder. They were lighter than the M54 types they replaced, which had the benefit of lowering the weight in the nose of the Z4 and so improving both handling and turn-in to some extent. The loss of weight was largely a result of using a magnesium cylinder block instead of the M54's iron block; in practice, only the outer block was

BMW ENGINE CODES

Since the 1960s, BMW's engine codes had been preceded by the letter M, which stood for Motor. However, by the turn of the century, the company had clearly decided not to take this set of numbers beyond 99 but rather to establish a new numbering system with a different prefix letter. The choice fell on the letter N, which was both logical and illogical: the letter actually stood for nothing at all, although it did follow M in the alphabet.

At about the same time, numbers in the E-prefix range used for whole-car projects were exhausted, and the company began to use an F prefix for its new models. E had stood for Entwurf (design or project), while F was simply the next letter in the alphabet.

MAKEOVER – THE 2006–2008 MODELS

The new N52 engines were concealed under sound-deadening cosmetic covers, which were quite different from those used on the earlier engines.

made of magnesium and there was an aluminium interior for the cylinders.

There were two versions of each 6-cylinder engine in the Z4 range, the differences lying in the software control system and in the inlet manifold. The smaller 2.5-litre type – the N52B25 type in BMW-speak – came with 180PS (177bhp) in the 2.5i models or with 218PS (215bhp) in the 2.5si types. Neither of these was sold in the USA, which instead had the lower-powered version of the 3.0-litre engine that was denied to ECE markets.

The larger 3.0-litre engine, or N52B30, went into the 3.0i models for the USA, when it had the same 218PS (215bhp) as the 2.5-litre engine for ECE markets, but a much higher torque output of 280Nm (210lb ft). This made the Z4 3.0i considerably quicker than the car it replaced, and official figures showed that it was more economical too. The more powerful engine, which went into 3.0si models for both ECE and US markets, came with 261bhp and 315Nm (232lb ft), which made it usefully quicker still.

All these engines came with a six-speed manual gearbox as standard, and the option of a six-speed automatic was available for the 6-cylinder types. A new Sport Automatic gearbox was available as an extra-cost option for the 2.5si and 3.0si models, and this came with paddle shifts on the steering wheel to provide more rapid and sporting shifts. This was the first time such a system had been available in a BMW, although aftermarket specialists such as Alpina had been offering paddle shifts for some time.

■ MAKEOVER – THE 2006–2008 MODELS

The Body Changes

The exterior facelift gave the car a lower, ground-hugging appearance, thanks to a new front bumper with a larger air intake. The apron now incorporated rectangular foglights, and there were new side reflectors (marker lights in the USA) in the front wheel arches. When the Xenon headlights were fitted, these now incorporated the much-liked 'angel eye' corona rings. From the rear, the revised cars looked wider and more muscular, thanks to a redesigned bumper and new tail lights with horizontal Z8-pattern 'light rods' for the turn signals. A new design of 17in wheel now became standard – although, as always, there were multiple extra-cost options – and inevitably there were some new paint colour choices as well. On the inside, the cars had new aluminium trim elements and an aluminium shift knob for automatic cars, plus more new colour choices.

The new coupé body was even stiffer than the exemplary roadster equivalent, with a torsional rigidity of 32,000Nm (23,600lb ft) per degree. The body had been planned from the start of work on the Z4 project, and that showed: it was clearly a far more carefully realized design than the 'bread-van' Z3 Coupé had been. It had a swooping roofline with a concave centre that journalists were prone to call a 'double-bubble' roof, although it was very different from the designs by Italian coachbuilder Zagato which had originally borne that name in the 1950s. It also had a hatchback to give access to a decently sized boot; later, it would become clear that this was a change from the original intention to have a fixed rear deck and an opening glass window panel to give access to the load area. A particularly neat touch was the way the fixed-roof body incorporated the 'Hofmeister kick', a traditional BMW feature, in the shape of its rear side windows.

ABOVE AND OPPOSITE, TOP: **The facelifted Z4 Roadsters were readily recognizable from the front thanks to a redesigned spoiler apron and the presence of side marker lights in the wheel arches. The car pictured is a 3.0i model.**

MAKEOVER – THE 2006–2008 MODELS

The top model of the revised range was the 3.0si, and this one carries the appropriate identification behind the front wheel arch.

■ MAKEOVER – THE 2006–2008 MODELS

The tail was also revised for the facelifted Z4s. Most obvious in this picture are the new light units, with horizontal 'rods' for the turn indicator segments. The third brake light, set into the 'hump' of the boot lid, now had a clear lens instead of a red one.

The rear apron of the facelifted cars was more angular than before, as is clear in this photograph. Note also the different lower lip.

MAKEOVER – THE 2006–2008 MODELS

BELOW AND RIGHT: These rear views of Z4 Coupés show a key difference between US and other models of the car. Both types have a red lens for the third brake light, but only the US-specification car has a red side marker light in the rear apron.

That boot was more than just a token, too, and BMW claimed that it was large enough to carry two golf bags. It had a fabric roller cover that could conceal a volume of 285ltr (8.6cu ft), and its maximum capacity without that cover in place was 340ltr (11.9cu ft). A further neat touch was that the tailgate release was concealed behind the BMW roundel at the rear of the car. Rather less neat was that the wing-mounted radio aerial of the roadsters was retained – an anachronism at a time when other fixed-roof BMWs had a neat multi-function 'shark's fin' at the rear of the roof.

As they had done with the Z3, BMW made the coupé body available only with the top engine options. In the case of the Z4, that meant the high-performance 6-cylinder from the M division (see Chapter 7) and the latest 3.0-litre engine. The first volume-production coupé was built on 10 April 2006, and the news that the concept seen at the Frankfurt Show in October 2005 really was becoming a production car was confirmed when the new models were displayed at the New York Auto Show later that same month. UK deliveries of Z4 Coupé models began in August 2006.

MAKEOVER – THE 2006–2008 MODELS

Features and Options

The revised Z4s once again came with a high level of standard equipment, which included a CD player, central locking, electric windows and air conditioning. Once again, run-flat tyres were standard, with ABS brakes, and the latest DSC+ suite of stability and traction control systems which included additional braking features such as pre-tensioning, brake drying, fade compensation, soft stop and hill start assistant. Safety equipment included airbags for both driver and passenger, together with knee airbags, side airbags and the pop-up rollover protection system.

BMW's latest safety thinking had also gone into the new two-stage Adaptive Brake Display, which was designed to reduce the risk of rear-end shunts. The theory was that whenever the driver applied the brakes hard (or if the ABS was activated), the illuminated areas in the rear lights would grow larger and following drivers would typically assume this to indicate an emergency braking situation and react accordingly, giving themselves a better chance of pulling up in time to avoid a collision. As before, the standard headlights on most models were halogen types, although the 3.0si (and M models) came with high-intensity bi-Xenon lights.

The standard trim level for the revised Z4s was known in some countries as the SE specification, and it came with 17in alloy wheels on all models. There were extra-cost alternatives, of course, and 18in M Double-spoke alloy wheels were fitted with the Sport option that was now made available with all engine types. On Coupé models, the Sport package also brought an Anthracite headlining, and on all models it came with BMW's DDC II (Dynamic Drive Control – see sidebar) stability control system. Then there was the M Sport suspension option, which lowered the car by 15mm from standard. That package brought with it half-leather sports seats, a more meaty three-spoke M steering wheel, and aluminium style trim panels for the cockpit.

The newly revised Z4 could also be had with a THX-certified sound system, the first of its kind from a German manufacturer. THX was a sound quality assurance system originally developed for the film industry, and the 430W Premium Sound System for the Z4 came with ten speakers, carefully positioned to give the best acoustic performance for the car's occupants. These consisted of two subwoofers with an output of 100W located behind the seats, two woofers each developing 40W at the front of the car, and six mid-range loudspeakers and tweeters. The system also included a seven-band graphic equalizer and a ten-channel digital audio amplifier and digital sound processor.

The most obvious changes in this interior shot are the control buttons on the steering wheel spokes and the six-speed gate marked on the gear shift grip. The foldaway navigation screen is clear on the top of the dashboard.

MAKEOVER – THE 2006–2008 MODELS

THE DSC SUITE

The DSC (Dynamic Stability Control) system came with a number of sub-functions, as follows.

ASC   Automatic Stability Control
Controls slip of the drive wheels by reducing engine output wherever required, applying the brakes selectively on a drive wheel about to spin, and thus stabilizing the car.

CBC   Cornering Brake Control
Reduces any inclination of the car to oversteer by controlling brake pressure asymmetrically whenever the driver applies the brakes slightly in a bend.

DBC   Dynamic Brake Control
Maximizes brake pressure whenever required, for example in an emergency braking manoeuvre, in order to keep stopping distances to a minimum.

DTC   Dynamic Traction Control
Enables the driver to improve traction at the touch of a button on surfaces with a low frictional coefficient.

Automatic Dry Braking
Optimizes the response of the brakes in the wet by keeping the brake discs dry for maximum efficiency.

Brake Standby
Helps to build up brake pressure more quickly whenever the driver lifts off the accelerator pedal rapidly, by automatically preloading the brake pads in position for braking.

Fading Compensation
Sets off any reduction of brake power by increasing brake pressure as a function of temperature.

Set-Off Assistant
Briefly applies the brakes when setting off on an uphill gradient to prevent the car from rolling back.

DYNAMIC DRIVE

BMW's Dynamic Driving Control (DDC) allowed the driver to change the programming of the transmission and steering to give the car more sporting dynamics. It had three prearranged settings: Normal, Sport and Sport +. Sport and Sport + modes sharpened the steering response and speeded up the accelerator response, and on cars with automatic or DCT gearboxes they also allowed the car to hold on to lower gears for longer for maximum acceleration while speeding up the gear changes themselves. The Sport + setting also disabled the DSC traction control system, providing Dynamic Traction Control (DTC) in its place.

DTC compensated for wheelspin, slowing a spinning wheel until it was able to regain traction and thus providing maximum grip and acceleration on poor surfaces. In particular, DTC could also allow greater slip on the rear wheels when that was the most appropriate way of maintaining traction.

On cars with adaptive dampers, DDC also adjusted these to give a firmer ride with the Sport and Sport + settings.

THE ICE AND NAVIGATION SYSTEMS

The Z4's ICE and navigation systems came in two levels, called Business and Professional, and either navigation system could be combined with a telephone installation as yet another optional extra.

The Business sound system featured a ten-channel audio amplifier with a total of ten loudspeakers. The Professional HiFi system gave improved sound through the use of special Carver technology.

The Business navigation system used a DVD with mapping for the whole of Europe, and could also control the onboard computer, radio and telephone. The Professional navigation system added an adjustable colour display.

■ MAKEOVER – THE 2006–2008 MODELS

What the Press Thought

Understandably, much of the press interest in the revised Z4 range was focused on the Z4 Coupé and the new M derivatives. *Autocar* took a brief look at a 3.0si Coupé for its issue dated 12 July 2006, and was impressed. 'Most of all it is the car's soul that will hook you,' they wrote.

> The Z4 Coupé is the new rogue in BMW's range, but a lovable one at that. . . . The 3.0si represents cultured power, emanating presence and authority like a well-tailored suit. . . . [The stiff bodyshell is] evident from the moment you commit the Z Coupé into a bend; there's no hesitation, no understeer, just satisfying balance. True, the run-flats rob a little composure and the steering doesn't have the right level of feel, but it remains an enthusiast's drive.

Clearly, the familiar flaws of those controversial tyres and electrically assisted steering remained unchanged.

There were other gripes, too.

> The Z4 Coupé is not without its faults; poor rear visibility, tyre noise and the use of some suspect materials all grate. But there's a lot to like, too: that splendid engine, the slick gear change, brakes that have a great feel – and even the semi-useful hatchback boot.

In the USA, *Car and Driver* pointed out the keen pricing that was an important factor in the new coupé's appeal in that country:

> Unlike Porsche with its Cayman and Boxster twins, BMW does not charge more for its Z4 coupé than its convertible. Prices for the 3.0si coupé start at $40,795, a $2000 savings over the Z4 3.0si ragtop and almost $10,000 less than the base Porsche Cayman.

The magazine liked the engine a lot because it 'makes incredibly smooth power through a slick-shifting six-speed manual or a six-speed automatic.' However, the car was far from ideal for everyday use:

> The Z4 coupé, as with the roadster, can be a chore to commute in . . . owing to heavy steering and a twitchy

The real E86 Z4 Coupé arrived with the facelifted cars in 2006. The wheels seen here were certainly much plainer than the ones seen on the Concept Coupé in autumn 2005, but they suited the car's lines rather well.

MAKEOVER – THE 2006–2008 MODELS

The coupé shape was well resolved, and much more satisfying than that of the Z3 Coupé, which had of course been a later 'conversion' of the Z3 Roadster bodyshell. These cars never carried model badges on their wings because there was only one variety available apart from the M derivative – the 3.0si.

tendency to be pulled around by pavement troughs and seams. The suspension is downright nervous on imperfect surfaces (and where are they perfect besides Germany?), requiring constant correction and allowing little relaxation. Were the Z4 ours to keep, we'd look for possible suspension tweaks or aftermarket bits that might settle it down.

Meanwhile, Evo magazine for September 2006 in the UK tried out the new fixed-roof car and liked it:

The Coupé instantly feels a different animal to the roadster: stiffer all round, but with the front feeling much more direct and eager to snuffle out an apex. Unusually for a small BMW, this means that on a bumpy B-road it's the front rather than the rear that commands your attention, the nose hunting out cambers and imperfections. It's not enough to slow you down, however, and the more you increase your speed, the more stability the Z4 seems to find.

Evo also wondered whether some of the expensive options were really worth having: 'I can't see any earthly reason why you would want the stiffer M Sports suspension, or any dynamic reason why you should spec rims bigger than the standard 17s.'

The new Coupé did not get all the press coverage, of course, and *BMW Car* magazine tried out a 2.0i Roadster for its April 2006 issue.

On the road, the car feels no slower than the 2.2i; . . . it's far from disappointing. . . . The noise from the Valvetronic four isn't quite the ticket, though. It's smooth enough and revs cleanly but it lacks the soulfulness and high-rev howl of a six – particularly with the lid down.

Even so, 'Front end grip is excellent and the car really does feel pointy. There's enough power to unstick the back end on a roundabout or tight bend if you're heavy footed and the car exhibits a fine balance when sliding.' Fuel consumption

MAKEOVER – THE 2006–2008 MODELS

was disappointing: 'We never saw over 29mpg despite the manufacturer's claim it'll do nearly 10mpg more than that on the combined cycle.' The low level of equipment that helped BMW achieve its attractively low showroom price was also a drawback. 'It is not a conspicuous bargain in the line-up but it represents decent value compared to the six-pots, if you are prepared to stay away from the goodies on the options list.'

In their August 2006 issue, *BMW Car* also had a view on the value of the 18in wheel-and-tyre combination in the Sport specification. In comparison with the 17in size that came with the SE specification, they felt that 'the trade-off in terms of grip is infinitesimal', and added: 'We'd wager that 99 per cent of drivers would be unable to detect the difference from the driver's seat.'

It was *BMW Car* again that published its thoughts based on long acquaintance with the 3.0si Coupé when it examined one as a used car buy in its March 2012 issue. The magazine concluded that it was probably a better buy than the equivalent Z4 M version of the Coupé: 'If you want a car with suspension rather than without, then the 3.0si is really your only choice.'

Production Changes, 2007–2008

The revised Z4s had been introduced so close to the normal start of the 2007 model year that no important changes were made at that point. However, from autumn 2006 an AUX input socket was added to the in-car entertainment system so that music from iPod and MP3 players could be fed through the car's amplifier and speakers.

When the Z4 had been introduced in 2002, BMW had anticipated that it would have a seven-year production life. In practice, its production would end in mid-2008 after just six years, and the last car would be built on 28 August 2008. This was not, though, the end of the Z4: the car's replacement for the 2009 season was also called Z4, and was known internally as the E89 type.

In anticipation that news of the replacement model would become public knowledge during the 2008 model year (as indeed it did), BMW provided interest in the existing models through special editions.

In the UK and other European countries, interest in the 2.0i models was boosted by the arrival of 2.0i Edition Exclusive and Edition Sport models in March 2008.

The BMW Individual scheme allowed buyers to create some very distinctive colour combinations, and also formed the basis of some of the company's limited-edition models. MAGIC CAR PICS

Fewer than 300 examples of these were planned. The Edition Exclusive models came with metallic paint, 17in Star Spoke alloy wheels, and Nappa leather upholstery plus high-gloss Piano Black interior trim from the BMW Individual range. The 2.0i Edition Exclusive cost £1,045 more than a standard production 2.0i model, but represented a customer saving of £1,835 over purchase of its special options individually. The five paint options were Montego Blue, Sapphire Black, Space Grey, Stratus Grey and Titan Silver.

The 2.0i Edition Sport also came with a choice of metallic paints, but with 18in Composite Star-spoke alloy wheels. The interior on these cars had sports seats upholstered

PRODUCTION OF Z4 E85 AND E86 MODELS, 2002–2008

Production of the E85 and E86 Z4 models was nowhere near as high as that of the Z3 models they replaced. In six years, a total of 197,950 Z4s of all types were built, for an average of 3,299 a year. By contrast, the Z3 had reached a production total of 279,819 in six years, giving a yearly average of 4,663.

Of the 197,950 Z4s built, 180,856 were Roadsters and 17,094 were Coupés.

Alpina worked their magic on the Z4 Coupé too, calling the result an Alpina Coupé S.

Z4 PERFORMANCE FIGURES, 2006–2008 MODELS

2.0i Roadster	0–100km/h (0–62mph)	8.2sec
	Maximum	137mph (220km/h)
2.2i Roadster	0–100km/h (0–62mph)	7.7sec
	Maximum	140mph (225km/h)
2.5 SE	0–60mph	7.1sec
	Maximum	142mph (229km/h)
2.5 Si SE	0–100km/h (0–62mph)	6.5sec
	Maximum	149mph (240km/h)
3.0si Roadster and Coupé	0–100km/h (0–62mph)	5.7sec
	Maximum	155mph (250km/h) (limited)

in Bi-colour New England leather, together with Bi-colour interior trim. Both features came from the BMW Individual range. The 2.0i Edition Sport was priced at £775 more than the standard production Sport model, but came with additions that would otherwise have cost £2,500. The five paint options on these cars were Black Sapphire, Carbon Black, Montego Blue, Space Grey and Titanium Silver.

Production of the first-generation Z4 models came to a close on 28 August 2008, when the last car rolled off the production lines at Spartanburg. It was a 3.0si Roadster painted in Space Grey, and was handed over to the Zentrum, the visitor centre and museum at the Spartanburg plant, where it went on display. It was a significant car in more ways than one, for it would be the last sports roadster to be built at the US assembly plant. The plan was for its replacement to be built in Germany, while the US factory focused on the model ranges that sold especially strongly in that country – the BMW X-series SUVs. In practice, the Z4's place on the assembly lines at Spartanburg would be taken by the new X3 model.

MAKEOVER – THE 2006–2008 MODELS

Z4 PAINT OPTIONS, 2006–2008 MODELS

The paints listed here are the standard showroom colours. It was of course possible to order colours from the BMW Individual custom-finishing catalogue at extra cost.

2006 model year

Colour	BMW code	Colour	BMW code
Alpine White III	300	Jet Black	668
Arktissilber Metallic	309	Monaco Blue Metallic	A35
Azuritschwarz Metallic	S34	Mondstein Metallic	S37
Black Sapphire Metallic	475	Montego Blue Metallic	A51
Blue Onyx Metallic	S11	Oxfordgruen II Pearl	430
Bright Red	314	Rubinschwarz Metallic	S23
Deep Green Metallic	A43	Sepang Silver Metallic	A32
Diopsidschwarz Pearl	A37, S44	Sterling Silver Metallic	A08
Estorilblau Metallic	335	Stratus Gray Metallic	440
Flamenco Red Metallic	470	Titanium Silver Metallic	354
Interlagos Blue Metallic	A30		

2007 model year

Colour	BMW code	Colour	BMW code
Alpine White III	300	Jet Black	668
Aventurinsilber Metallic	S58	Monaco Blue Metallic	A35
Azuritschwarz Metallic	S34	Mondstein Metallic	S37
Black Sapphire Metallic	475	Montego Blue Metallic	A51
Blue Onyx Metallic	S11	Oxfordgruen II Pearl	430
Bright Red	314	Rubinschwarz Metallic	S23
Deep Green Metallic	A43	Sterling Silver Metallic	A08
Diopsidschwarz Pearl	A37, S44	Stratus Gray Metallic	440
Estorilblau Metallic	335	Titanium Silver Metallic	354

2008 model year

Colour	BMW code	Colour	BMW code
Alpine White III	300	Jet Black	668
Aventurinsilber Metallic	S58	Monaco Blue Metallic	A35
Azuritschwarz Metallic	S34	Mondstein Metallic	S37
Black Sapphire Metallic	475	Montego Blue Metallic	A51
Blue Onyx Metallic	S11	Oxfordgruen II Pearl	430
Bright Red	314	Rubinschwarz Metallic	S23
Deep Green Metallic	A43	Sepang Bronze Metallic	A32
Diopsidschwarz Pearl	A37, S44	Space Gray Metallic	A52
Imola Red	405	Stratus Gray Metallic	440
Interlagos Blue Metallic	A30	Titanium Silver Metallic	354

Z4 SPECIFICATIONS, 2006–2008 MODELS

Engines

2.0-litre
Type N46B20 4-cylinder petrol
1995cc (84 x 90mm)
Twin ohc, chain-driven
4v per cylinder
Double-VANOS variable valve timing, Valvetronic control and DISA variable inlet manifold
Seven-bearing crankshaft
Compression ratio 10.5:1
Bosch engine management system
Three-way catalytic converter standard
150PS (148bhp) at 6,200rpm
200Nm (148lb ft) at 3,600rpm

2.5-litre
Type N52B25 6-cylinder petrol
2497cc (82 x 78.8mm)
Twin ohc, chain-driven
4v per cylinder
Double-VANOS variable valve timing, Valvetronic and DISA
Seven-bearing crankshaft
Compression ratio 11.0:1
Siemens engine management system
Three-way catalytic converter standard
2.5i version:
180PS (177bhp) at 6,500rpm
230Nm (169lb ft) at 3,500rpm
2.5si version:
218PS (215bhp) at 6,500rpm
250Nm (184lb ft) at 2,750–4,250rpm

3.0-litre
Type N52B30 6-cylinder petrol
2996cc (85 x 88mm)
Twin ohc, chain-driven
4v per cylinder
Double-VANOS variable valve timing, Valvetronic and DISA
Seven-bearing crankshaft
Compression ratio 10.7:1
Siemens engine management system
Three-way catalytic converter standard
3.0i version (USA only):
218PS (215bhp) at 6,600rpm
280 Nm (210lb ft) from 2,500–3,500rpm
3.0si version (ECE and USA):
265PS (261bhp) at 6,600rpm
315Nm (232lb ft) at 2,750–4,250rpm

Transmission
Six-speed manual gearbox standard
　　　　Ratios 4.35:1, 2.5:1, 1.66:1, 1.23:1, 1.00:1, 0.85:1
Six-speed automatic gearbox optional
　　　　Ratios 4.17:1, 2.34:1, 1.52:1, 1.14:1, 0.87:1, 0.69:1

Axle ratio
3.23:1　　(2.5i manual)
3.93:1　　(3.0i manual)

Suspension, steering and brakes
Front suspension with MacPherson struts, double wishbones, coil springs and anti-roll bar
Rear suspension with multiple links, coil springs and anti-roll bar
Rack-and-pinion steering with 14.2:1 ratio and standard electric power assistance
Disc brakes all round, with twin hydraulic circuits; ABS standard; 2.5i with 286mm ventilated front discs and 280mm ventilated rear discs; 3.0i with 300mm ventilated front discs and 294mm ventilated rear discs

Dimensions

Overall length	4,090mm (161.0in)
Overall width:	1,780mm (70.1in)
Overall height:	1,300mm (51.2in) – Roadster
	1,285mm (50.6in) – Coupé
Wheelbase	2,495mm (98.2in)
Front track	1,473mm (58in)
Rear track	1,523mm (60in)

Wheels and tyres
8J x 17 alloy wheels with 225/45 ZR 17 run-flat tyres
8J x 18 alloy wheels with 225/40 R 18 run-flat tyres

Unladen weights

2.0i Roadster	1,295kg (2,855lb)
2.2i Roadster	1,325kg (2,921lb)
2.5 Roadster	1,335kg (2,921lb)
2.5 SE	1,360kg (2,998lb)
2.5 si SE	1,360kg (2,998lb)
3.0i Roadster	1,365kg (3,009 lb)
3.0si Roadster	1,385kg (3,009 lb)
3.0si Coupé	1,395kg (3,075lb) with manual gearbox

CHAPTER SEVEN

THE M DIVISION'S Z4

BMW's claim when the Z4 was launched that there was no M derivative planned was scarcely believable, and within four years the M division had not one but two versions of the Z4 M ready for sale. So had anything really changed in the meantime, or had the company simply been toying with its customers in autumn 2002?

The answer to that question is not quite straightforward. On the one hand, the sales and marketing people were undoubtedly disappointed that the Z4 did not sell better in its first few years, and realized that the range needed an additional fillip to help sales along. On the other hand, the M division's engineers probably had a good look at the Z4 early on to see what they could do with it if they were asked – and were only too pleased to be asked some time around 2004 to turn their ideas into a production-ready car.

There were certain elements that fell naturally into place. The E46 M3 was already using an M-developed version of the straight-six engine, and this certainly had enough power to deliver the expected performance. However, a different gearbox would have to be used because the M3's six-speed type did not fit into the space available in the Z4. The suspension could easily be tautened to provide handling appropriate

Imola Red paint was exclusive to the M division's cars, and it suited the Z4 M Roadster perfectly. Note that the M cars did not have the side marker lights in their front wheel arches that characterized the facelifted mainstream cars.

THE M DIVISION'S Z4

The deeper front air dam developed for the M cars had a large central air intake, flanked on each side by brake cooling scoops. The twin kidney grilles were also set deeper into the bodywork than on mainstream models.

to an M car, and it would be a simple matter to develop a suitable wheel and tyre combination. However, special sizes of run-flat tyres were probably going to prove too expensive. There was also the problem that the electric power steering on the standard cars did not seem to give the right amount of feedback, and M customers would want changes here.

The programme to develop a Z4 M must have begun with the Roadster and then expanded to include a Coupé. The BMW board was initially not keen on the idea of a coupé model because the M Coupé version of the Z3 had not been a very strong seller. However, the M division's engineers went ahead and built a prototype anyway, and the story goes that the board liked it so much when it was demonstrated to them that they approved the Z4 M Coupé for production.

In practice, the two models were introduced separately. The M Roadster was formally announced at the North American International Auto Show in Detroit in January 2006, and the Coupé Concept already seen at the Frankfurt Motor Show was shown with it. Production of roadsters began that month and the first cars were delivered in late March. The M Coupé was announced at the Geneva Motor Show in March; production then began in June and deliveries followed shortly afterwards. The whole programme had been preceded by a succession of careful hints and 'leaks' since the end of 2005, in order to build up customer anticipation.

THE Z4 M ROADSTER

Mechanical

It was no real surprise that the new M Roadster should draw very heavily on components already in production for the M3, which by this stage was based on the E46 3 Series. The M division's engineers borrowed not only the M3's engine but also elements of its suspension, brakes and power-assisted steering.

Starting with the engine, the M Roadster came with a new version of the S54B32 straight-six, which was very slightly less powerful than the same engine in the E46 M3 thanks to the shorter and more restrictive exhaust system needed for the Z4. Nevertheless, the Z4's version of the engine came with more computing power than the M3 version, thanks to a new MSS70 management system capable of processing 64 million calculations per second as compared to the 25 million calculations per second available from the M3's MSS54 system.

This engine actually had different ratings for the US and ECE models, mainly because the exhaust catalysts had to be located differently on the US engines to give faster warm-up characteristics. Both versions of the engine were redlined at 8,000rpm; US engines had 330bhp at 7,900rpm and 262lb ft

THE M DIVISION'S Z4

The rear of the **Z4 M Roadster** had the same new light units and clear third brake light as the mainstream cars. Where it differed was in the shape of the apron, which had a unique air diffuser and of course cut-outs for the four tailpipes so characteristic of the **M** division's cars. The famous **M** badge with its tricolour accompaniment was on the left of the boot lid.

of torque at 4,900 rpm, while the ECE engines had 343bhp and 365Nm (269lb ft) of torque.

Both US and ECE engines drove through the same gearbox, and the M division's engineers had found the solution to their transmission problems in a new six-speed manual from ZF called the Type H. This was the only option available on the M Roadster, and it had ratios very similar to those of the Getrag gearbox in the M3. It transmitted power to a tall 3.62:1 final drive that came with an M Differential Lock as standard. This was essentially a modern version of the traditional limited slip differential; entirely mechanical in operation, it was activated by a difference in rotational speed between the two rear wheels. This difference pressurized a viscous silicone fluid, which then operated a multi-disc clutch that directed more power to the wheel with the greater traction. In order to accommodate the M Differential Lock, the M Roadster had a larger and stronger rear subframe than the mainstream Z4 models.

As for the suspension, the basic layout already used on the Z4 models was well up to the tasks that the M model would demand of it. So the MacPherson struts and multi-link rear end remained in place, although there were many changes in detail. For a start, the ride height was lowered overall by 10mm (0.39in) and there was more negative camber for the wheels. The springs and dampers were rated specifically for the M model, and all wheel bearings were uprated. The Z4's battery was already mounted at the rear, and remained there in the Z4M to give the best possible front-to-rear weight balance.

The longitudinal links in the rear suspension were special, and there were fatter anti-roll bars front and rear. At the front end, the lower aluminium control arms were changed for items similar to those on the E46 M3 and the steering knuckles were bolted directly to the front struts. The front track was half an inch wider than on mainstream Z4s and, most importantly for steering feel, the electric power assistance of the mainstream Z4s had gone. In its place was a conventional hydraulic system that borrowed most of its components from the E46 M3, although the characteristics of the power steering pump had been modified to suit the lighter roadster.

The brakes were very different from those of the parent car, having been uprated with components from the Competition package developed for the E46 M3 (and made standard on the M3 CSL). Not only were the discs larger than those of the mainstream Z4, but they also had a two-

No car from the M division would be complete without its special alloy wheels and uprated brakes. Both can be seen clearly here.

piece 'compound' design that greatly improved heat dissipation under heavy braking. The steel discs themselves – cross-drilled and ventilated, of course – had aluminium hubs to which they were connected by stainless steel pins. These large brakes nestled behind the M division's distinctive M Double-spoke wheels (Style 224 in the catalogues), which had an 18in diameter, with 8in rims at the front and 9in rims at the rear.

The M Roadster also came with the expected battery of electronic traction and stability control systems. The 'umbrella' system was DSC+, which had several components. Dynamic Traction Control (DTC), Dynamic Brake Control (DBC), and cornering stabilization could all be disabled by a dashboard switch, but other components were permanently active. These were brake fade compensation (which increases servo pressure to adjust for rising brake temperatures); brake standby (which prepared the system for sudden braking if there was sharp lift off the accelerator); brake drying (activated by the rain sensor, this briefly brought the pads close to the discs in order to remove any water); and start-off assistant (which briefly applied the brakes when the pedal was released to prevent the vehicle rolling backwards on a hill).

THE S54B32 ENGINE

The S54B32 engine used in the M versions of the Z4 was the final evolution of the iron-block S50 straight-six that was first introduced in ECE versions of the E36 M3 in 1992. The S54 derived from an evolution of this engine, the 3.2-litre S50B32 that was used in ECE-specification Z3 M models and in the later ECE-specification E36 M3. Key features of the S54 engine were:

Larger bores (87mm instead of 86.1mm) to give 3246cc
One-piece aluminum head casting to reduce weight
Higher compression ratio (11.5:1 instead of 11.3:1)
Different camshafts
Finger-type rocker arms for reduced reciprocating mass and friction
Double-VANOS continuously variable valve timing system
BMW/Siemens MSS70 engine management system
Electronic throttle activation with two M Dynamic Driving Control response modes
Scavenger-type oil pump to maintain lubrication during heavy cornering

■ THE M DIVISION'S Z4

These two views show the 3.2-litre **S54** engine under the bonnet of the **Z4 M**. This **M** division engine also saw service in the **E46** M3 cars, where a less restrictive exhaust system allowed it to develop a few more brake horsepower.

THE M DIVISION'S Z4

Appearance

The Z4 M was distinguished visually from other Z4 roadsters by a number of subtle differences that made up a distinctive package. At launch, it was available in a choice of eight colours, of which three were exclusive to the M division's products. Once production had become established, additional colours from the BMW Individual catalogue became available in June, together with two special-order options.

At the front, the twin black 'kidney' grilles were set deeper into the bodywork than on mainstream Z4s, and there was a deeper and more aggressive bumper valance panel with a large central air intake feeding more air into the engine and brake cooling scoops on either side. The bonnet, too, was unique, with a pair of styling lines running from front to back that hinted distantly at an old-style power bulge. At the rear, there was no boot-lid spoiler – although one had certainly been tried because one of the cars at the Z4 M press launch had one – but there was an aerodynamic diffuser that extracted hot air from around the finned differential. There was also the M trademark – four exhaust tailpipes.

From the side, the clearest distinguishing features were the 18in M Double-spoke alloy wheels, but for the avoidance of doubt there was also an M division badge behind the BMW roundel on each front wing. A third M badge was located on the left-hand side of the tail – slightly surprisingly, because other M models all had such badges on the right at the rear. What could not be seen was the flat underfloor that improved high-speed airflow under the car and reduced axle lift.

The basic interior layout was the same as in other Z4s, but of course the M division had made sure that buyers of an M Roadster would get something special. The seats were M Sport types and they were upholstered in leather; an Extended Leather option at extra cost added matching leather to the centre console, upper door panels, windscreen frame, sun visors and rollover bars. The colour options naturally included some that were unique to the M division.

There were special features for the controls, too. All cars had an M steering wheel with a thicker rim and tricolour stiching, a leather-trimmed shift grip with an illuminated shift pattern, and a special instrument pack. The dials on this had special graphics with red needles and there was also an oil temperature gauge in place of the usual coolant temperature dial. The speedometer, which carried an M logo, read to 300km/h (or 180mph) and the rev counter had a vari-

The roundel indicator light units were the same as on other Z4s, but behind them was once again the famous M badge.

■ THE M DIVISION'S Z4

Branded sill plates and M Sport seats with more supportive bolsters were characteristic of the Z4 M. This car has the Extended Leather option, with leather on the dash top, console and rollover hoops.

BMW M enthusiasts revel in the little details that set the M division's products aprt from their mainstream equivalents. There are several in evidence here: note the M steering wheel, the carbon fibre-look trim, the M branded instrument dials, and the M gearshift grip, which was internally illuminated when the car's lights were on.

able LED redline which moved round the dial as the engine warmed up, discouraging the driver from using higher engine speeds until it had reached operating temperature. There was of course a Sport button, but pleasingly its settings were preprogrammed and there was no need to go through the tedious routine of choosing personalized settings demanded by some other BMWs. Sport gave direct access to noticeably sharpened accelerator response, and no Z4 driver could have wished for more.

As was expected of cars from the M division, the door sill plates were chromed and carried the M logo. Then there were special interior trim finishes, which were Hexagon aluminium, Black Carbon Structure leather (a matt leather with a carbon-fibre weave) and Madeira walnut. A self-dipping M rear-view mirror was also standard.

Despite the high level of standard equipment, there was still an options list. Available at extra cost in most markets were heated seats, Business or Professional satellite navigation systems and a body colour aluminium hardtop. Also on offer (although again depending on market) were Park Distance Control, cruise control, power-folding exterior mirrors, an auto-dimming interior mirror, power front seats with driver's side memory, a Bluetooth phone interface, and various audio and speaker systems including Professional Logic7. In the USA, a Premium package was available, consisting of cruise control, power memory seats, upgraded audio, and the BMW Assist system.

Inevitably, the Z4 M was speed-limited to 155mph (250km/h), a maximum which was also attainable by other models within the Z4 range. So the spotlight was thrown

Strong colours suited the M cars just as much as the mainstream Z4s. The convertible roof was of course power operated, as on other models.

This low-angle shot gives a good impression of the Z4 M's power potential – but of course the car was normally viewed from further off the ground.

THE M DIVISION'S Z4

onto its accelerative ability, and of course the car was decisively quicker than any mainstream Z4 model of the time. Acceleration from zero to 100km/h (62mph) took exactly 5.0sec, which translated to a 4.7sec 0–60mph time (4.8sec for US-model cars). Happily for BMW, these figures also made it slightly quicker than the Porsche Boxster S (and, in Coupé form, similarly quicker than the Porsche Cayman S).

What the Press Thought

Not surprisingly, press reports on the Z4 M Roadster tended to focus on the engine. When Autocar magazine tried an example for its issue dated 12 April 2006, it reported that 'the BMW's engine is about as peaky as the Bonneville salt flats. Here's a power-house that delivers substantial slam as well as monumental spin . . . sustained linear shove is a speciality.' However, the news was not all good, because 'the M-motor, while fabulously flexible, is boomy below 2000 revs . . . and the usually quick and positive gearchange can be annoyingly sticky if you're not in a hurry.'

Equally unsurprising was that testers compared the car to its obvious rival, the highly regarded and somewhat less expensive Porsche Boxster S. *Autocar* found that the BMW had its own distinctive character:

> *There's a lean, raw simplicity to the Z4 M that's missing from the subtle, mutli-layered agenda of Porsche's rival and, in many ways superior, Boxster S. The Z-car feels brutally quick in a way that the Porsche never quite does.*

Somewhat surprisingly, specialist magazine *BMW Car*, which might have been expected to favour the BMW, felt that the Porsche was ultimately a more satisfying car. Even so, it found the Z4 M impressive. In its issue of April 2006, the magazine reported that

> *The engine dominates proceedings from the off . . . [and] is happier once it's up past 2,000rpm. Keep it pinned and the acceleration just builds and builds as the engine turns up the volume in an utterly addictive fashion.*

As for the car's dynamic qualities:

> *The weighting is perhaps a little lighter than it could be, but detailing and feel are good and despite the heavy straight six up front there's little understeer unless you are trying hard.*

Production Changes

The Z4 M Roadster was available for only just over two full seasons, so there were few production changes. As already noted, new paint and interior options were introduced in June 2006. Then for 2007 (beginning on production in October 2006), an auxiliary input was added to the BMW Business audio head unit, a TPM (Tyre Pressure Monitor) system replaced the earlier FTM (Flat Tyre Monitor), and High-Definition radio became a factory-fit option for countries where HD broadcasts were available.

These details apart, the only production changes were to the paint, upholstery and interior trim options (see below).

Z4 M COUPÉ

The Z4 M Coupé shared its basic bodyshell with the Z4 3.0i Coupé and inherited its distinctive visual characteristics from the Roadster. So the car benefited from the parallel bonnet creases that added character; the deeper front air dam and special rear valance; and the four polished tailpipes.

Most of its mechanical specification also came from the Roadster, although the stiffer bodyshell had allowed the M division to quicken the steering ratio; the different weights also called for a thicker rear anti-roll bar and slightly stiffer dampers than in the Roadster. The differential, too, was altered, to make the car turn in better. Even so, the fixed-roof bodyshell was just 5kg (11lb) heavier than the open version, which was not enough to do damage to acceleration figures or to the maximum speed of the car. At the launch, BMW made much of the fact that these minor differences made the M Coupé quicker than the Roadster around the Nordschleife at the Nürburgring, and also faster than an M3 Coupé on the same track.

Just as the M Roadster had to tackle competition from the Porsche Boxster S, so the M Coupé had a Porsche model in its sights – this time, the fixed-roof Cayman S coupé. The BMW was in fact both quicker and cheaper than its Porsche rival, but that did not give it automatic domination of its

THE M DIVISION'S Z4

Like the mainstream coupés, the **Z4 M Coupé** had a red lens for its third tail light. This is a **US**-specification model, with marker lights in the rear bumper apron. The radio aerial was the same as on Roadsters, although other fixed-roof **BMW**s normally had a shark's fin receiver module mounted at the rear of the roof. WIKIMEDIA/IAN MUTTOO

market sector; the Nissan 350Z coupé was another formidable contender, and that was a lot cheaper than the BMW.

The European media launch for the Z4 M Coupé was held in Portugal, and those who attended were treated to an opportunity to try the cars at the limit on the Estoril racetrack. In the USA, the car was introduced on 27 May 2006 and customer deliveries began immediately afterwards. Right-hand-drive Britain had to wait until August for its first deliveries.

Production Changes

Like its Roadster sibling, the Z4 M Coupé changed very little over its short production run. The 2007 models shared changes with the Roadsters, gaining the auxiliary radio input, the TPM system and the factory-fit High-Definition radio option.

There were changes to the paint options, too. Monaco Blue metallic paint had not been available on US-specification cars in the beginning, although it could be had on ECE cars.

■ THE M DIVISION'S Z4

THE MOTORSPORT COUPÉ

Carefully timed to reinforce the excitement around the launch of the new M Coupé, BMW Motorsport announced the availability of a special ready-to-race model on 7 March 2006. This was the first two-seater model that BMW Motorsport had offered for racing enthusiasts, and was available to order from May 2006.

The car was designed to appeal to both wealthy individuals who wanted to race a Z4 M Coupé and professional touring and production car racing teams around the world. This was a very special racing machine and came at a high price – in Europe, approximately €250,000, plus VAT where applicable; in Britain, £233,500; and in the USA $391,025.

The engine in the Motorsport Coupé was a further development of the Z4 M's 3.2-litre 6-cylinder, delivering around 400PS (395bhp). The suspension had been modified with knowledge gained from the 2001–2002 M3 GTR project, and the car came with a number of race-adjustable components. As produced in Munich, it weighed 1,200kg (2,643lb) with its driver and was equipped with a 120ltr (30gal) fuel tank to suit endurance racing.

A Z4 Motorsport Coupé won the Silverstone Britcar 24 Hour endurance race for Duller Motorsport in 2006, crewed by Dieter Quester, Dirk Werner, Jamie Campell-Walter and Tim Mullen. The following year, the car won again, this time with the same crew except for Tim Mullen, who was replaced by Johannes Stuck.

Introduced in 2006, the Motorsport Coupé was a specialist development of the Z4 M Coupé, intended to appeal to professional touring and production car racing teams. Its engine delivered around 400PS (395bhp).

THE M DIVISION'S Z4

If the **Z4 M** was not enough, there was no shortage of aftermarket volunteers to improve it. This coupé was worked on by Hamann Motorsport, who made sure it looked the part as well, with a neat rear wing spoiler.

■ THE M DIVISION'S Z4

From October 2006, however, it became available on US cars as well. A year later, Space Grey metallic paint replaced Silver Grey metallic for the 2008-model Z4 M Coupés.

What the Press Thought

There was general agreement in the printed media that the Z4 M Coupé was a much better driver's car than its Roadster sibling. In a retrospective look at the two cars, the March 2010 issue of *BMW Car* loyally concluded that 'the driving experience is very similar but it's the Coupé that pips the Roadster in terms of handling; though the differences are very subtle and you wouldn't be disappointed with either.'

Even so, *Autocar* had been slightly disappointed in the Coupé when it tested one for its issue dated 24 May 2006. Although it had a number of good points, there was a nagging suggestion that 'it wasn't as it should be'; there was a suggestion that somehow the M division had pulled its punches and could have made the car even better. Among the tangible negatives were 'some pretty cheap cabin materials that have no place in a car costing £41,285'.

The fixed-roof car was certainly not spacious: 'the cockpit is on the cramped side of snug . . . yet the very intimacy of this environment is irresistible. . . . from the very start, this is a car you want to wear.' But the car was certainly a better drive than the Roadster: 'Unlike the Roadster, it doesn't require you to be brutal with it; you just need to treat it with a firm hand.'

BMW Car tested an early example for its July 2006 issue, and revelled in the car's good points.

> *There's a nice rorty note to the exhaust that builds in intensity as you climb your way round the tacho. Blasting past a sheer rock face with the windows open, the noise ricocheting back in the cabin is intoxicating and savage. The bellowing crescendo as you head towards 8,000rpm and get the full 343bhp is totally addictive.*

This, though, was not really different from the Roadster experience. It was the handling that made the Coupé a more rewarding car to drive:

> *If you really take the M Coupé by the scruff of the neck and start to hurl it around, it transforms into a 340-bhp go-kart. You can feel the extra stiffness translating into pin-point precision.*

The steering was good but not quite perfect; it was 'light but weights up well at speed and manages to convey all the detail you need without ever feeling really lucid'. The ride was distinctly firm, though, and even 'choppy at times. . . . for those wanting a comfy cruiser, you'd be advised to look elsewhere.' Yet for all its savage performance, questionable ride and sharp handling, it was also a civilized machine. In fact, 'it's generally smooth and docile around town.'

That small cabin again occasioned comment. 'The cabin is best described as snug,' wrote *BMW Car*. 'Taller drivers really have to duck their heads in, and . . . there's not too much head room.' And there was a 'lack of rearward visibility . . . the rear screen becomes something of a letterbox for taller drivers.'

The Z4 M Coupé still felt good when *BMW Car* took a retrospective look at it in March 2010, well after production had ended, although praise was tempered by criticism. On the positive side,

> *the Z4 M responds instantly to steering inputs and while the steering is a touch light there's plenty of feel. Grip and traction are both exemplary and in the dry you really have to be pushing hard to unstick the rear.*

On the negative side:

> *It's not without its faults, starting with the ride. On the smoothest of roads and when pressing on, the suspension is superb. . . . However, on the sort of roads most of us have to deal with on a day-to-day basis it is excessively firm. The car skips and bounces over rough surfaces with mid-corner bumps occasionally throwing the nose off course with the rear struggling to put the power down on bad roads. . . . The other major problem with the Z4 M is the huge amount of road noise those tyres generate; it's bad in the Coupé and worse in the Roadster and makes the car a tiresome long-distance companion, seriously limiting its cruising abilities.'*

And, once again, the lack of space in the cabin was a problem: 'The non-adjustable wings on the sport seats also mean that if you're of larger build you'll find them a squeeze.'

THE 2006 MILLE MIGLIA CONCEPT COUPÉ

At the 2006 Mille Miglia classic road race event, BMW unveiled a special concept coupé that was intended to pay homage to the BMW 328 coupé that had won the race in 1940. The timing of this announcement was undoubtedly arranged to give an additional promotional push to the facelifted Z4 range introduced in spring 2006.

The 2006 Mille Miglia Concept Coupé used the drivetrain of a 3.2-litre Z4 M, but it was never intended to race. It was designed by Z4 designer Anders Warming and had some deliberate similarities to the original 328 coupé as well as some reflection of the 'flame-surfacing' of the Z4; Warming also used a traditional clay-and-plaster design process to create the car instead of more modern computer-generated images.

The bodywork itself was made from carbon-fibre reinforced plastic, and the concept car was 23cm longer, 14cm wider and 4cm lower than a Z4 M Coupé. To provide entry to the cockpit (and to deliver the 'wow' factor expected in a concept car), the whole cabin top section, including windows, hinged upwards at the back. The cockpit was largely trimmed in stainless steel, undyed leather and Lycra fabric. Finishing touches were 20in alloy wheels with 245/40 R 20 tyres and an LED headlight panel.

The car now belongs to the collection of the BMW Museum in Munich.

The Mille Miglia Concept Coupé was based on the Z4 M but was used as a promotional tool when that car was introduced. WIKIMEDIA/BISER TODOROV

■ THE M DIVISION'S Z4

(continued from previous page)

Though an extremely attractive design, the Mille Miglia concept was never allowed to influence the design of the production **Z4** – not even that of the second-generation models introduced two years later. WIKIMEDIA/THESUPERMAT

Z4 M ROADSTER PRODUCTION FIGURES

Type	Specification	Production dates	Total
BT91	European (ECE), LHD	January 2006 to July 2008	1,425
BT92	European (ECE), RHD	January 2006 to July 2008	921
BT93	North American, LHD	February 2006 to August 2008	3,041
		Grand Total	5,387

Z4 M COUPÉ PRODUCTION FIGURES

Type	Specification	Production dates	Total
DU91	European (ECE), LHD	April 2006 to July 2008	1,714
DU92	European (ECE), RHD	April 2006 to June 2008	1,052
DU93	North American, LHD	April 2006 to August 2008	1,815
		Grand Total	**4,581**

The DU93 (North American) production figures break down as follows: 377 cars in 2006, 1,188 cars in 2007, and 250 cars in 2009.

Z4 M PAINT OPTIONS

M Roadster and M Coupé models were available with the same paint options. Note that Coupé production began in April 2006 but that the colour options were those listed here as from June 2006.

January 2006 to May 2006

Eight paint colours were available. Three of these (Imola Red, Interlagos Blue and Sepang Bronze) were exclusive to the M division. Monaco Blue metallic was not available in the US market.

Alpine White III	300	Monaco Blue metallic	A35
Black Sapphire metallic	475	Sepang Bronze metallic	A32
Imola Red II	405	Silver Grey metallic	A08
Interlagos Blue metallic	A30	Titanium Silver metallic	354

June 2006 to August/September 2007

Twelve paint colours were available. Three colours (Imola Red, Interlagos Blue and Sepang Bronze) were exclusive to the M division. Two colours (Midnight Blue and Ruby Black) came from the BMW Individual options list. Two more (Carbon Black and Phoenix Yellow) were available to special order only. Monaco Blue metallic was not available in the US market.

Alpine White III	300	Monaco Blue metallic	A35
Black Sapphire metallic	475	Phoenix Yellow metallic	445
Carbon Black metallic	416	Ruby Black metallic	S23
Imola Red II	405	Sepang Bronze metallic	A32
Interlagos Blue metallic	A30	Silver Grey metallic	A08
Midnight Blue metallic	453	Titanium Silver metallic	354

(continued overleaf...)

■ THE M DIVISION'S Z4

(continued from previous page)

October 2007 to August 2008
Eleven paint colours were available. Three colours (Imola Red, Interlagos Blue and Sepang Bronze) were exclusive to the M division. Two colours (Midnight Blue and Ruby Black) came from the BMW Individual options list. One (Carbon Black) was available to special order only. Monaco Blue metallic now became available in the US market.

Alpine White III	300	Monaco Blue metallic	A35
Black Sapphire metallic	475	Ruby Black metallic	S23
Carbon Black metallic	416	Sepang Bronze metallic	A32
Imola Red II	405	Space Grey metallic	A52
Interlagos Blue metallic	A30	Titanium Silver metallic	354
Midnight Blue metallic	453		

Z4 M UPHOLSTERY AND TRIM OPTIONS

M Roadster and M Coupé models were available with the same upholstery and trim options. Note that Coupé production began in April 2006 but that the options were those listed here as from June 2006.

Upholstery
Upholstery was in leather as standard, and the choice lay between the standard type and the extended type (which covered additional areas; see text).

January 2006 to May 2006
There were six options, all unique to the M division cars.

Black Nappa leather	LSSW	Imola Red Nappa leather	LSIM
Black extended Nappa leather	LTSW	Light Sepang Bronze Nappa leather	LSA8
Dark Sepang Brown Nappa leather	LSD6	Light Sepang Bronze extended Nappa leather	LTA8

June 2006 to August 2008
There were eighteen options, of which six were unique to the M division cars and the other twelve came from the BMW Individual catalogue; the Individual options included four two-tone choices. Note that the BMW Individual options were not available in some countries.

Amarone Nappa leather	LPF2	Estoril Blue and Anthracite New England leather	NBC3
Amarone extended Nappa leather	LLF2	Imola Red Nappa leather	LSIM
Black Nappa leather	LSSW	Imola Red and Anthracite New England leather	NBC9
Black extended Nappa leather	LTSW	Light Sepang Bronze Nappa leather	LSA8
Caramel Nappa leather	LPCR	Light Sepang Bronze extended Nappa leather	LTA8
Caramel extended Nappa leather	LLCR	Phoenix Yellow and Anthracite New England leather	NBC4

(continued opposite...)

(continued from previous page)

Champagne Nappa leather	LPCM	Silverstone and Anthracite New England leather	NBC5
Champagne extended Nappa leather	LLCM	Syrah Blue Nappa leather	LPF3
Dark Sepang Brown Nappa leather	LSD6	Syrah Blue extended Nappa leather	LLF3

Trim

There were four trim options, of which the three unique to the M division were available throughout production and the fourth (Piano Black) was from the Individual catalogue and became available in June 2006. Note that the BMW Individual option was not available in some countries.

Brushed Aluminum	4AD	Madeira Walnut wood	4ME
Carbon Leather	4MY	Piano Black	4ML

Z4 M SPECIFICATIONS, 2006–2008 MODELS

Engine
Type S54B32 6-cylinder petrol
3246cc (87 x 91mm)
Twin ohc, chain-driven
4v per cylinder
Double-VANOS variable valve timing
Seven-bearing crankshaft
Compression ratio 11.5:1
BMW/Siemens MSS70 engine management system
Catalytic converters standard
ECE version:
343PS (338bhp) at 6,900rpm
365Nm (269lb ft) at 4,900rpm
US version:
330bhp at 6,900rpm
355Nm (262lb ft) at 4,900rpm

Transmission
Six-speed ZF Type H manual gearbox
    Ratios 4.35:1, 2.50:1, 1.66:1, 1.23:1, 1.00:1, 0.85:1,

Axle ratio
3.62:1

Suspension, steering and brakes
Front suspension with MacPherson struts, coil springs and 27mm anti-roll bar
Rear suspension with multi-link layout of semi-trailing arms, separate springs and dampers, and 21.5mm (Roadster) or 22.5mm (Coupé) anti-roll bar
Rack-and-pinion steering with 15.4:1 ratio (Roadster) or 14.5:1 ratio (Coupé) and hydraulic power assistance
Disc brakes all round, with twin hydraulic circuits; ABS standard; 345mm (13.7in) diameter cross-drilled 'compound' discs at the front and 328mm (12.9in) at the rear.

Dimensions
Overall length	4,113mm (161.9in)
Overall width	1,780mm (70.1in)
Overall height	1,300mm (51.2in) – Roadster
	1,285mm (50.6in) – Coupé
Wheelbase	2,497mm (98.3in)
Front track	1,486mm (58.5in)
Rear track	1,516mm (59.7in)

Wheels and tyres
8J x 18 M Double-spoke alloy front wheels, with 225/40 ZR 18 tyres
9J x 18 M Double-spoke alloy rear wheels, with 255/40 ZR 18 tyres

Unladen weights
Roadster	1,450kg (3,197lb)
Coupé	1,455kg (3,208lb)

CHAPTER EIGHT

THE SECOND GENERATION Z4 – THE E89 MODELS

For the third generation of its 'affordable' roadster, BMW planned from the start to make the car more comfortable and luxurious, with extra features that would justify higher prices. Inevitably, the car would be rather softer than those which had gone before it, and more of a boulevardier. Yet, at the same time, the challenge was to maintain performance while suffering the inevitable weight penalties of extra equipment. In addition, exhaust emissions and fuel consumption both had to be lowered in line with the latest customer expectations.

There were also criticisms to be countered. The cabin of the E85 and E86 Z4 models was rather cramped, and large people complained of insufficient headroom and shoulder room; some also found it difficult to get into and out of the car. So extra size was clearly going to be necessary because the skin panels were already wrapped quite tightly over the mechanical elements on the E85 and E86 models. In the end, the BMW designers added 148mm (5.83in) to the length of the old car and 9mm (0.35in) to the width. Within these dimensions, they added larger door apertures and 20mm

The lead designers on the E89 project were both women. Juliane Blasi (left) was responsible for the exterior and Nadya Arnaout (right) ran the interior design team.

THE SECOND GENERATION Z4 – THE E89 MODELS

A full-size clay of the E89 is seen here during development in the design studio. Note the highlight 'edges' on the wall drawing.

(0.79mm) more shoulder room, plus more elbow and head room. All this was achieved on the same wheelbase as the E85 and E86 models and while retaining the classic roadster proportions of a long bonnet and short tail, with the driver sitting just ahead of the rear wheels.

Much of the design work for project E89 was done during 2006. At this stage, BMW's chief designer was still Chris Bangle (who would be succeeded by Adriaan van Hooydonk in 2009), and he ran a classic design competition within his studio. Several designers put forward sketches and ideas in the usual way, but Bangle encouraged two of his female designers to see if they could produce better solutions than their male colleagues. In the end, they did, and Juliane Blasi was appointed lead exterior designer for the E89, with Nadya Arnaout running interior design.

The exterior design chosen for production was very much an evolution of the Anders Warming design for the E85 and E86 models, with a straight lower body swage line, a more clearly defined rear wing line and a different treatment for the side gills. It still reflected Bangle's 'flame-surfacing' ideas, but was less extreme than its predecessor, notably lacking the stylized Z-like pressing on each front wing and adding feature lines to the bonnet, which had been very plain and flat-looking on the earlier Z4. New headlights linked the design firmly to other members of the BMW family then in production or scheduled for it, with a wrap-around 'eyebrow' style.

Perhaps the most significant change for the E89 models was one dictated by manufacturing considerations. There had been both Roadster and Coupé versions of the Z3 and first-generation Z4 models, but the additional manufacturing costs of having two bodyshells in production were unwelcome. So the new E89 was designed as a roadster with a retractable hardtop, thus allowing one bodyshell to meet the requirements of those who wanted a closed car as well as those who wanted an open one. BMW may have felt a little uncomfortable about following a trend they had not started themselves – the Mercedes-Benz SLK models had been built with retractable hardtops since 1996 – but they made sure that their version of the design was as advanced as it could be. The aluminium hardtop for the E89 was created as a two-piece structure with electro-hydraulic operation that could open or close the roof in 20 seconds. There were a few drawbacks, the most obvious one being a loss of boot space when the roof was down: the 310ltr (11cu ft) available with it in the up position was reduced to just 184ltr (6.5cu ft).

Body strength and crash safety were, as always, important considerations in the design of the E89. Among the features incorporated in the new shell were diagonal cross-members to add reinforcement to the doors and protect the occupants against side impacts. Meanwhile, the bumpers were given reversible aluminium impact absorbers at the front

■ THE SECOND GENERATION Z4 – THE E89 MODELS

THIS PAGE AND OPPOSITE: **This early sDrive 35i model demonstrates the E89's party trick: the two-piece folding roof could be raised or lowered in just 20 seconds – and the car looked just as attractive when closed as it did when open.**

THE SECOND GENERATION Z4 – THE E89 MODELS

■ THE SECOND GENERATION Z4 – THE E89 MODELS

and steel impact absorbers at the rear, and were able to withstand impacts of up to 2.5mph (4km/h) without damage.

The interior was laid out to provide more cabin space and more luxury than the earlier two-seater roadsters. Nadya Arnaout's design also provided some welcome visual interest on the dashboard, where the vast blank sweep of the earlier Z4 had attracted criticism. This time, visual relief came from four circular heating and ventilating controls in the centre. Leather was to be standard for the upholstery on all but the entry-level models, and overall the comfort of the cabin was much improved. To compensate for the loss of boot space when the folding hardtop was down, the E89 was designed with a through-loading feature, although in production this became an extra-cost option. Another thoughtful touch was a profusion of cupholders, stowage nets and cubbies, although these too would be relegated to an extra-cost Storage package.

The E89's cabin was also crammed full of the latest technology. So the car was designed with an electronic parking brake, which was not only a fashionable feature but had the practical benefit of saving the space otherwise occupied by a handbrake lever. There were no fewer than four airbags: one each at the front for the passenger and the driver, plus head and upper body airbags to cushion the head, ribcage and pelvis area. And, inevitably, there was an iDrive system with an 8.8in display screen that folded down into the dash top, plus all the latest BMW information and entertainment software that had appeared on the F01 7 Series cars earlier in 2008.

The lead chassis engineer was Heinz Krusche, whose task was made easier by being able to use off-the-shelf suspension hardware that was shared with the latest 1 Series and 3 Series cars. In line with the aim to make the E89 a more luxurious car, the dampers chosen were softer than those on earlier BMW two-seaters, but to satisfy customers who wanted a more traditional sports car feel, an Adaptive M Sport suspension package was prepared. This came to market as an extra-cost option (of course) and brought a 10mm

The E89's dashboard was much more attractive than that on its predecessor. The two-tone colour treatment on this early right-hand-drive car showed the design at its best; the iDrive screen folded away into the dash top when not in use.

THE SECOND GENERATION Z4 – THE E89 MODELS

A six-speed manual gearbox was standard, and the iDrive control, electronic parking brake and DDC switches were all conveniently located around the gear shift.

(0.39in) lower ride height and electronic damper control with three settings. Steering was once again to be electrically power assisted, despite rumblings of discontent about this feature in the E85 and E86 models; it eliminated the engine power losses through a conventional hydraulic pump and also allowed fine-tuning of steering response.

There was certainly no shortage of engines already in production from which the E89 project team could choose. For the initial release, the engineers chose updated versions of two engines already available in the E85 and E86 models, plus one newer power plant to give interest at the top of the range. The carry-over engines were the 2.5-litre and 3.0-litre versions of the 6-cylinder N52 family first introduced in 2004. The new engine would be from the turbocharged N54 family, which had made its debut in 2006. Other engines could be introduced later to meet demand.

These first engines had to fall into line with the requirements of BMW's Efficient Dynamics programme. So all those supplied with manual gearboxes were designed to have the automatic Stop/Start system that saved fuel by shutting the engine down during prolonged stops, such as at traffic lights. Efficient Dynamics also ensured that manual-transmission cars would have a gear-change indicator light on the dash to encourage the driver to change up at the optimum point and so save fuel – and that all E89s would have a Brake Energy Regeneration system that converted energy from braking into electrical power for the battery and put the alternator out of circuit during normal running to reduce the load on the engine.

There were plenty of existing electronic driving aids to choose from, too, and it was only to be expected that Dynamic Stability Control (DSC) would be standard equipment. The version engineered into the E89 included Cornering Brake Control (CBC), Brake Assist (BA) and Dynamic Brake Control (DBC), and Hill-Start Assistant was selected as a feature added to top models only. The DSC system could be fine-tuned by the Dynamic Drive Control (DDC) system, which was made standard for the first time on a BMW roadster. Operated by a Sport button next to the gear shift, this acted on the accelerator, the steering, the change points of the automatic transmission (if fitted) and the damper settings (when Adaptive M Suspension was fitted) to sharpen the car's responses and give a more sporting drive. Dynamic Traction Control (DTC) also allowed increased wheel slip to optimize acceleration in certain types of driving conditions.

As already explained (see Chapter 7), this third-generation two-seater would not follow its predecessors on the production lines in South Carolina, but would instead be built in Germany. So, beginning in 2007 as the E89 project reached production readiness, BMW invested €130 million in extending their Regensburg factory so that they could build the car there.

THE SECOND GENERATION Z4 – THE E89 MODELS

The First E89s, 2008

There had been no particular reason to worry about the state of the global economy when BMW had started work on the design and development of the E89 models. The whole programme was arranged well in advance so that the car could be announced at the end of 2008, and volume production was planned to build up gradually to ensure showroom supplies by the early summer of 2009. In practice, the E89 was launched into a major economic downturn that had hit the auto industry hard during 2008.

It was hardly the best time to be introducing a new roadster, a car that was likely to be an optional purchase rather than an essential one. Yet the programme was so advanced when the economic downturn began that BMW really had no choice but to go ahead as planned and to hope that the global economy would recover. So the new E89 roadster was announced to the media on 13 December 2008 and, like the car it replaced, carried the Z4 name. It was shown in public for the first time at the North American International Auto Show in Detroit during January 2009, alongside the new Mini Convertible from BMW, and entered volume production a month later. Invited media representatives had a chance to try it out at a ride-and-drive exercise held in the Spanish resort of Alicante, and the global roll-out followed in May.

As with the previous Z4, the launch models were all 6-cylinder types. These were the 2.5-litre sDrive23i, the 3.0-litre sDrive30i and the twin-turbocharged sDrive35i – names that helped to prove that BMW's badges were no longer a clear indicator of engine size but rather of market positioning. Even the designations themselves were slightly odd, without the decimal point that would indicate engine size – and that sDrive prefix was explained away by BMW as indicating that the vehicles had rear-wheel drive.

The E89, seen here in right-hand-drive form for the UK, had more immediate presence than the car it replaced. The sculpted lines of the bonnet were a major improvement in this respect.

THE SECOND GENERATION Z4 – THE E89 MODELS

From the rear, there was no indication of the engine variant; the tail bore only a Z4 badge.

Obvious rivals for these new models were seen as the Mercedes-Benz SLK and the Audi TT – although there was (somewhat surprisingly) no diesel engine to counter the success of the Audi TT TDI Quattro, and there never would be a diesel E89 Z4. As for a model to rival the Porsche Boxster, which had been the nemesis of the earlier Z4, that could wait until later.

The main aim of the new engines had been to reduce emissions and fuel consumption with minimal loss of performance, and in that aim BMW had certainly succeeded. Although all three models accelerated with slightly less urge than the older Z4 models they replaced, they did not feel slower to drive and all boasted very respectable fuel economy – around 41mpg (6.9ltr/100km) for the two smaller-engined cars and around 33mpg (8.6ltr/100km) for the top model sDrive35i. As the E89 Z4 was heavier, model for model, than its predecessor, that was no mean achievement.

All three variants of the new Z4 came with a six-speed manual gearbox as standard, which was wholly adequate for most types of driving, although a six-speed Sport Automatic with steering-wheel paddle shifts was available as an option and was a better choice if the car was going to be used a lot in town traffic. The sDrive35i model was very quick indeed, and accelerated very nearly as fast as the earlier M versions of the E85 and E86 Z4. Twin tailpipes were one easy way of recognizing this top model of the E89 range.

All three models came with 17in Star-spoke wheels as standard, featuring run-flat tyres once again: there was simply no room for a spare wheel in the tightly packaged E89 bodyshell, despite the increase in size over its predecessor. A Tyre Pressure Monitoring system was standard, by way of compensation, and came with an audible warning to indicate sudden deflation. There were 18in M Star-spoke wheels to be had, and these came as part of an extra-cost M Sport package, which also added M Sport suspension, M aerody-

■ THE SECOND GENERATION Z4 – THE E89 MODELS

The first cars all had 6-cylinder engines, and it was impossible to tell which engine was fitted just by a casual glance under the bonnet, where plastic cosmetic and acoustic covers dominated the scene.

namic body styling, high-gloss Shadowline exterior trim, and M badges on the wings. The package also brought M logos on the door sills, an anthracite coloured headlining, Sport seats with special Kansas leather upholstery, Carbon Aluminium cabin trim and an M Sport steering wheel. Also exclusive to E89 Z4s ordered with the M Sport package was the option of Melbourne Red metallic paint.

Leather upholstery was standard on all but the entry-level models, and there was an extra-cost Extended Leather option as well, in the usual BMW fashion. Above that came a Design package option, which brought Ivory White nappa and alcantara upholstery with Fineline anthracite wood trim and (optionally) Havanna Brown exterior paintwork.

The drive to make the second-generation Z4 a more luxurious car than its predecessor had led to the new models coming with a temptingly high specification as standard. Even entry-level models had electric windows, headlight washers, Xenon headlights with a Welcome Light and Daytime Running Lights, a heated rear window in the folding hardtop, and a soft-close bootlid. Inside the cabin, owners found ISOFIX fittings for a child seat, an on-board computer, Tyre Pressure Monitoring, a multi-function Sport steering wheel, DDC, an auxiliary infotainment input, plus BMW Emergency Call and BMW TeleServices in countries where these systems were supported. A DAB tuner was also standard in countries where DAB radio broadcasts were available.

THE OPTIONS LIST AT LAUNCH

It was typical of BMW to offer an extensive options list for E89 Z4 buyers right from the start of production. So the options listed when the cars were new included:

Adaptive Headlights
Auto-dim rear view mirror and exterior mirrors
Comfort Access (key fob not required to lock or unlock doors and boot, or operate windows; also included remote operation of the convertible roof)
Cruise Control (with brake function)
Driver's side electric seat adjustment memory
Extended Storage
Folding Exterior Mirrors
Heated steering wheel
Media package (including BMW Apps, BMW Online Services, Information Plus, Internet, BMW Professional Multimedia – Navigation System, Remote Services, TV Function and Voice Control; the internet connection was not available in all markets, and notably not in the UK)
Wind Deflector
Windscreen shade band (grey)

THE SECOND GENERATION Z4 – THE E89 MODELS

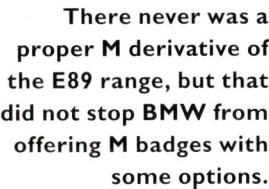

The M Sport body kit was available across the range, and is seen here on an sDrive 30i model. The side repeater indicator ahead of the front wheel arch makes clear that this is a facelift or 'LCI' car.

There never was a proper M derivative of the E89 range, but that did not stop BMW from offering M badges with some options.

■ THE SECOND GENERATION Z4 – THE E89 MODELS

Among the benefits of the retractable folding roof was that it allowed the car to have a proper glass rear window. With the roof up, boot space was quite generous for a two-seat roadster . . .

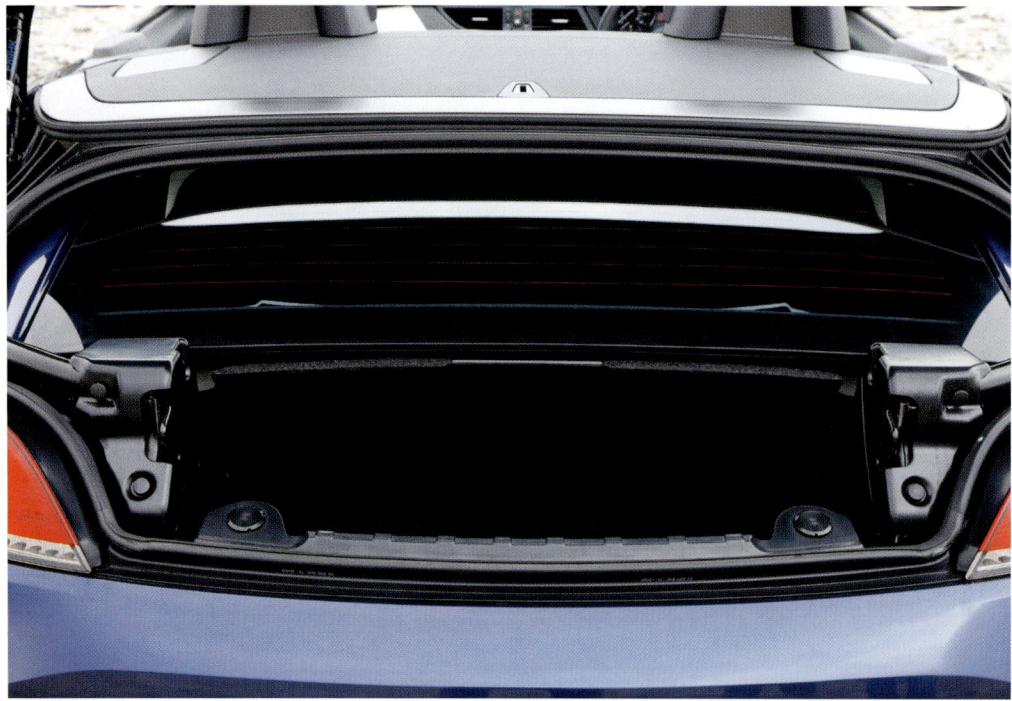

. . . although with the roof stowed away, the boot space shrank quite dramatically.

'There's no doubt about it, the Z4 has grown up,' reported *BMW Car* magazine after attending the media launch just outside Benidorm in Spain.

Whereas the original model was stiffly sprung and edgy when driven hard, this new one has been engineered to offer a much more refined driving experience. . . . [It all] suggests BMW has GT aspirations for this car.

THE SECOND GENERATION Z4 – THE E89 MODELS

The 2010 Model Year – an M Substitute

The absence of an M derivative from the initial release of E89 models was barely worthy of comment because it was common BMW practice to let a new model find its position in the marketplace before introducing an ultimate performance derivative. Besides, this was not a time to expect a hugely expensive top model: the economic climate would simply not support it, and that appears to have been one reason why aftermarket specialist Alpina never did develop a version of the E89 Z4.

However, it was not long before the stories began to circulate that there would be no M derivative of the E89 because the latest M division engine (in the M3) was a V8 – and that it could not be persuaded to fit into the E89's engine bay. That story was proved to be false when BMW announced a V8-powered GT3 variant for specialist competition use in 2010 but, one way or the other, there never would be an M derivative of the E89 Z4.

Nevertheless, BMW did their best to provide a substitute. That substitute was the sDrive35is, which was introduced in autumn 2009 for the 2010 model year. Essentially, it was a 35i model with a transient overboost feature that allowed additional torque to be generated briefly without risk to the engine. Electronics permitted a boost in power between 1,500rpm and 4,500rpm for seven seconds after every gear change under full throttle. This allowed the torque to reach 500Nm (370lb ft) for between one and two seconds at a time, giving an extra 50Nm (37lb ft) over the standard rating of 450Nm (332lb ft), but the full 500Nm was available only in the five upper gears. This feature gave the new car simply ferocious acceleration, and some commentators worried that this model was too powerful for its chassis – a criticism that some had also levelled at the sDrive35i model.

There was quite a lot more to the sDrive35is than clever electronic engine tuning, though. The only gearbox choice was a seven-speed DCT (Double-Clutch Transmission), and there were sharper suspension and steering settings and a special twin exhaust system tuned to give a sound that would satisfy any devotee of the M division's products. The model came as standard with the M Sport package of aerodynamic addenda, part-electric Sport seats, anthracite headlining and aluminium carbon trim.

Of course the sDrive35is also came with 18in wheels and the Adaptive M Sport suspension as standard. All cars

THE Z4 GT3

The special motorsport version of the E86 Z4 M Coupé introduced in 2006 had done a good job in maintaining a high-performance image for the car. BMW decided to follow it with a similar ready-to-race derivative of the E89. The car was prepared to meet the contemporary FIA GT3 regulations and was introduced in 2010.

It was powered by the P65B44 4.4-litre V8 engine from the M3 GTS, race-tuned to deliver 515PS (508bhp) at 9,000rpm and driving through a six-speed Hewland/X-trac sequential gearbox to a mechanical limited-slip differential with its own oil-to-air cooler. The car's structure incorporated ultra-lightweight carbon-fibre reinforced plastics, which reduced its overall weight to approximately 1,190kg (2,624lb). Although the overall outline of the Z4 GT3 was instantly recognizable as that of the production E89 Z4, a huge double-deck rear wing spoiler made for a very obvious difference. There was also a front aerodynamic splitter, while a set of winglets on the front wings provided additional downforce at speed.

Examples of the GT3 proved competitive in their first year of racing in the FIA GT3 Championship. One car won the Dubai 24 Hour endurance event, and Need for Speed Team Schubert finished second in the 24 Hours of Spa-Francorchamps event during 2011. In Japan, Nobuteru Taniguchi and Taku Bamba took their Z4 GT3 to the championship of the GT300 class in the 2011 Super GT season.

came with metallic paintwork and Extended Lighting, plus Kansas Leather upholstery and special floor mats with an sDrive35is logo.

The new model succeeded in giving BMW a credible competitor for the Porsche Boxster at the top end of its Z4 range, but the effects of the 2008 economic crisis were still reverberating around the world. *BMW Car* magazine summarized the position neatly when it reported that UK sales for the 2010 calendar year (which included half the 2010 model year and half the 2011 model year) were just 2,500 cars – a figure that compared poorly with the 4,300 E85 and E86 Z4 models sold in the 2007 calendar year.

155

■ THE SECOND GENERATION Z4 – THE E89 MODELS

The top model of the E89 range was the sDrive35is, which came with the M Sport body kit as standard. This BMW press photograph admirably captures what the car was all about.

The special rear apron and diffuser of the M Sport body kit added both distinction and interest at the tail of the car.

Hidden, as usual, under plastic covers, the engine of the sDrive 35is was a twin-turbocharged 6-cylinder with a special transient overboost system to improve acceleration.

THE SECOND GENERATION Z4 – THE E89 MODELS

Carbon-aluminium interior trim, a 35is logo on the floor mats, and the **M** logo on the sill plates, all helped to make the interior of the top model **E89** special.

Model designations were carried on the front wing below a **BMW** roundel, but the names were certainly not the best that the **BMW** marketing department had ever dreamed up.

■ THE SECOND GENERATION Z4 – THE E89 MODELS

The economic climate was not encouraging for the aftermarket specialists, and Hamann began working with the E89 very cautiously at first, offering a range of attractive wheel styles like those seen here.

However, AC Schnitzer decided to commit to a more comprehensive E89 improvements programme early on, and its ACS4 model was ready by the end of 2009. Note the discreet two-part boot-lid spoiler.

THE SECOND GENERATION Z4 – THE E89 MODELS

A TUNER'S E89 INTERPRETATION

Inevitably, the aftermarket tuning specialists who make their living by wresting more performance out of production BMWs turned their attention to the new Z4 in the hope of attracting custom once the economic recession had passed. Hamann Motorsport began somewhat cautiously with a range of special alloy wheels; Alpina never did work on the E89; but one company that was quick off the mark with a modified car was AC Schnitzer.

The ACS4 3.5i Turbo was based on an sDrive35i model. Electronic engine tuning plus a more free-flowing exhaust system boosted power to 360bhp at 5,850rpm and 384lb ft of torque between 3,000 and 4,750rpm. 'The power increase of 54bhp is impressive,' wrote *BMW Car* in its January 2010 issue, 'but it's the 89lb ft gain that's most important.' The standard BMW engine tune actually gave more torque lower down the rev range, but 'by the time the engine's spinning over 2,400rpm, the Schnitzer black box provides significantly more twist all the way to the redline. . . . Give it plenty of beans and it's quicker than just about anything I've ever driven.' Top speed, unhampered by the factory-specification limiter, was 176mph (283km/h) and the 0–62mph (0–100km/h) sprint was despatched in 4.9sec.

The Schnitzer conversion was also 'a lot more composed than the standard car', thanks to special springs and big 20in five-spoke alloy wheels with 9in front rims and 10in rears. Visual changes to the body were dominated by an extended front spoiler incorporating a large chromed air intake with a deeply slatted version of the standard grille above it. Two different tail spoilers could be had, and there were new front wing panels incorporating very stylish angled air outlets with bright metal strakes to give them definition.

2011 – 4-cylinder Models

Few people doubted that 4-cylinder models would join the E89 range eventually, and in late 2011 they did so. More surprising was that the new sDrive20i and sDrive28i actually replaced existing 6-cylinder models, the sDrive23i and sDrive30i respectively, which went out of production.

Both of the new 4-cylinder cars in fact had the same 2.0-litre engine, designated N20, which brought a collection of new technology to the Z4 range. The N20 engine had an aluminium block with iron cylinder liners created by means of a thin film deposition technology. It featured both Double-VANOS and Valvetronic technology, together with the latest Bosch GDI (Direct Gasoline Injection) fuel system using a high-pressure (200 bar) fuel pump driven by the exhaust camshaft.

Twin balancer shafts were used to reduce vibration, and to reduce piston friction the centre line of the crankshaft was offset from that of the cylinders – the first time BMW had designed an engine with this feature. To meet the requirements of BMW's Efficient Dynamics policy, the N20 also had an electric coolant pump (which reduced power drain on the engine) and an automatic Stop/Start system. But most importantly for lovers of acceleration, the engine had a twin-scroll turbocharger (and was branded as a TwinPower Turbo engine in consequence). In practice, this meant that the turbocharger had two sets of inlets and nozzles, one set for normal running and the other angled to give fast response with minimal turbo lag.

The sDrive20i became the new entry-level model. It was slightly slower than the sDrive23i, which it replaced, taking 6.6sec (as against 6.3sec) to hit 60mph from rest and peaking at 142mph (228km/h) as opposed to 150mph (242km/h). It was less powerful, too, with 184PS (181bhp) as against 204PS (201bhp) in the older car, but the highlight was in the enhanced torque delivery of the 4-cylinder engine, which achieved 270Nm (199lb ft) as opposed to the 250Nm (184lb ft) of the sDrive23i, and did so across a much wider rev range.

The engine in the sDrive28i also brought welcome benefits. Like the sDrive30i model it replaced, the car was limited to a maximum of 155mph (250km/h), so the drop in maximum power to 245PS (241bhp) from the earlier car's 258PS (255bhp) was academic. However, the new 4-cylinder engine again delivered more torque across a wider rev range, allowing the car to accelerate to 60mph in just 5.5sec; the older 6-cylinder had needed 5.8sec.

159

■ THE SECOND GENERATION Z4 – THE E89 MODELS

THE 328 HOMMAGE

In 2011, BMW once again used its two-seat roadster as the basis of a dramatic concept car. This was the 328 Hommage, designed to commemorate the seventy-fifth anniversary of the legendary BMW 328, which had dominated its racing class in the later 1930s.

The fully drivable concept featured lightweight carbon fibre reinforced plastic both in its body structure and its cabin interior. Notable features were the leather straps running across the bonnet (the original 328 had needed them to hold the bonnet sides in place at speed) and two-part alloy wheels, which visually recalled the steel discs of the original 328.

The 328 Hommage was first shown at the 2011 Rolex Monterey Motorsports Reunion and later that year appeared at the Pebble Beach Concours d'Elegance. It had no discernible effect on the development of the E89 Z4 range but was widely admired as a showcase for BMW's design skills. The car now belongs to the BMW Museum.

The 328 Hommage was based on the running-gear of the E89 Z4, but more for convenience than anything else. This attractive evocation of the great **BMW sports racers of the 1930s** was never intended to influence the design direction of the E89 itself.

THE SECOND GENERATION Z4 – THE E89 MODELS

BMW claimed that the new turbocharged 4-cylinder engines retained high-performance characteristics entirely suited to the Z4 but allied them to lower exhaust emissions. As for fuel economy, both engines averaged just over 41mpg (6.90ltr/100 km), which was pretty much the same as the 6-cylinders they replaced. It was very much a win-win solution – except that the 4-cylinder engines were undeniably less pleasant to listen to than the smooth sixes that had for so long been a BMW characteristic.

2012 – Zagato Concepts and Motor Sport Cars

The Zagato Coupé and Roadster

The Italian design consultancy Zagato, which had evolved from the famous coachbuilder of the same name, had never worked on a BMW in its ninety-year existence. However, BMW chief designer Adrian van Hooydonk was friendly with Zagato chief designer Norihiko Harada, and as a result of discussions between the two men, Andrea Zagato suggested building a show car based on the E89 Z4.

The BMW Zagato Coupé was first seen in public at the internationally renowned Villa d'Este concours event held at Lake Como in Italy in May 2012. The car attracted a great deal of favourable comment, and this prompted BMW and Zagato to build a second show car, this time as a Roadster. The BMW Zagato Roadster was created in an astonishingly short six weeks and was displayed in public at the Pebble Beach Concours d'Elegance in the USA during August 2012.

The E89 in Motor Sport

This was a period when BMW focused quite hard on promoting the Z4 range. While the two Zagato cars were attracting welcome attention, BMW was also preparing to take the E89 range into motor sport – especially in the USA. In recent years, the company's efforts in motor sport had been focused on the M3 in GT and GT2 versions, and this car had earned them team and manufacturers' titles in 2011 and 2012, a drivers' championship in 2011, GT class wins in the 12 Hours of Sebring race of the

Just about recognizable as a Z4, this is one of the GTE racers run by Turner Motorsport in US events.

161

■ THE SECOND GENERATION Z4 – THE E89 MODELS

THE ZAGATO Z4 CONCEPT CARS IN DETAIL

The BMW Zagato Coupé was hand-built around the mechanical elements of the E89 Z4. Zagato 'signed' it by creating the mesh of the twin-kidney grille out of multiple small letter Zs. These had a matt finish, contrasting with bright chrome Zs on the air intakes.

The coupé body recreated the famous Zagato 'double-bubble' roof of the 1950s – a feature that had also inspired the shape of the E86 coupé. It was painted in bright red Rosso Vivace, a multi-coat polychromatic paint that depended on a black primer coat, a layer of metallic silver, and six thin coats of red with two clear coats to add lustre. This had the effect of changing colour with the light, running all the way from nearly black to a brilliant red. The car also featured transparent rear panels with a dark tint, a tinted rear window and tail lights behind black tinted glass, while matt colours on the rear diffuser's edge, the 19in wheels and the tailpipes provided visual contrasts.

Interior trim depended on shades of grey with red contrast stitching, with the Zagato Z embroidered into the seats. The car was equipped with a hat bag and travel bag.

The BMW Zagato Roadster had the same grille design as the Coupé, with 'razorlight' headlights incorporating an LED light strip set into the matt surface above the lights themselves.

This time, the 'double-bubble' roof shape was incorporated into a fairing which ran to the rear of the car. The body was finished in another polychromatic paint, this time a brilliant grey that changed from dark grey to light silver. The interior this time was trimmed in black, with brown contrast stitching and a strip of brown leather running from the instrument panel, over the door sills and around behind the seats to cover the rollover bars.

Zagato's first design for the Z4 turned the car into a striking fastback coupé that was still recognizable as a derivative of the E89. Note the Zagato signature Z on the front wing.

THE SECOND GENERATION Z4 – THE E89 MODELS

The two Zagato concepts are seen together here; they shared front end details.

The Zagato Roadster was another fine design, but it came too late in the E89's production life to have any influence on the way the car would develop.

Zagato made few changes to the cabin of the roadster, although the choice of materials and colours was distinctive. The car had an automatic gearbox.

163

THE SECOND GENERATION Z4 – THE E89 MODELS

THE SECOND GENERATION Z4 – THE E89 MODELS

ALMS (American Le Mans Series) in 2011 and 2012 and multiple victories in the Intercontinental Le Mans Cup in Europe. For the 2013 season, however, the racing M3s would give way to new racing Z4s.

It was not at all surprising to discover that the new 'works' Z4 was to be a derivative of the special Z4 GT3 car that had been raced by privateers since 2010. Needless to say, BMW had been keeping a close eye on the privateers' progress and had no doubt learned a few things from their experience with the car on the tracks.

The new car was developed with an LM GTE specification, with a particular eye on the ALMS but also for other GTE class events. Most of its differences from the GT3 car lay in aerodynamics; the GTE used the same front splitter but had some major changes at the wheel arches to improve airflow around the front wheels. At the rear, the GTE racer also had much wider bodywork, a single-deck wing spoiler instead of the double-deck type of the GT3 car, and a less aggressive diffuser. Although the GTE car had a 4.4-litre V8 engine similar to that of the GT3, considerable reworking allowed it to produce up to 500PS (493bhp) at a lower 7,500rpm.

For competition in the USA, BMW entrusted the Z4 GTE to its long-time collaborators, Rahal Letterman Lanigan (RLL) Racing. It made its debut at the 2013 12 Hours of Sebring event, when the two cars entered ran competitively, handling extremely well and even leading their class at times, but were hindered late in the race by suspension problems. A 1-2 finish followed at the 2013 Long Beach Grand Prix, and then a second win at Lime Rock Park.

The Z4 GTE never quite achieved what BMW had hoped for it in US motor sport events. When the Tudor United Sports Car Championship replaced ALMS in 2014 (by merging with the Grand Am Series), the RLL Z4 GTEs ran in the GTLM (GT Le Mans) class. Both that year and in 2015, they showed extremely well but finished both seasons in second place to Porsche rivals. In 2014, US BMW performance tuners Turner Motorsport also campaigned a Z4 GTE in the Tudor United Sports Car Championship. Modified to suit the regulations of the GT Daytona class, the car earned the Drivers' Championship title for its driver, Dane Cameron.

Action at a pit stop: this is one of the Team RLL Z4 GTEs that just failed to conquer the Porsche opposition in the Tudor race series in the USA.

165

■ THE SECOND GENERATION Z4 – THE E89 MODELS

2013 – the Life Cycle Impulse

BMW started using the acronymn LCI to describe midlife facelifts for its cars during 2008. It was a peculiarly tortured euphemism for a facelift, the letters standing for Life Cycle Impulse. For the E89 Z4, the LCI was due during the 2013 season, and was actually announced in March that year.

BMW presumably thought that major changes would not be cost-effective as there were surprisingly few changes of any kind for the 2013 models. One worthwhile change was to the steering, where the 'feel' was improved. A new and lower-priced entry-level derivative made its appearance and was badged as an sDrive18i. This took the number of models up to five, as the existing range of sDrive 20i, 28i, 35i and 35is was carried over. For the first time in the Z4 range, 4-cylinder engines now outnumbered the 6-cylinder types.

The new sDrive18i model was yet another car with the twin-scroll turbocharged 2.0-litre engine, now detuned electronically to deliver just 156PS (154bhp) with a flat torque curve of 240Nm (177lb ft) between 1,250rpm and 4,400rpm. The car needed 7.6sec to reach 60mph and peaked at 137mph (220km/h), and it looked exactly like its 4-cylinder siblings except for the model designation mounted next to the gills on the front wings. Those who drove one and were familiar with other models in the Z4 range could not help feeling that the sDrive18i felt a little underpowered; this 4-cylinder was definitely in the boulevard cruiser mould rather than a powerful sports car.

Once prices had been announced, it became clear that the sDrive18i was a determined attempt to undercut the price of the Mercedes-Benz SLK 200, the entry-level model in its maker's range. Although prices varied around the world, depending on equipment levels, in the UK the BMW was considerably cheaper. That detuned engine alone could not of course justify the lower price to BMW's accountants: the lower power was really no more than a way of differentiating the new model from its more expensive siblings. The real cost savings came elsewhere: the car had single-zone air conditioning instead of the new dual-zone type introduced on other 2013-model Z4s, and also lacked the rain sensor feature with automatic headlight activation, again new for 2013.

No automatic gearbox option was offered for the sDrive18i, although all the other models in the E89 range could have it. On the 2013 models, the original six-speed type gave way to a new ZF eight-speed automatic, which offered smoother changes thanks to smaller gaps between

Headlights with corona rings were a distinguishing feature of the facelifted cars that arrived for the 2013 model year.

Few changes were made to the E89s after their facelift in 2012. This 2015-model sDrive 35is shows that the cars still looked good, especially with strong colours.

the ratios. As far as BMW was concerned, this was a Sports Automatic, and in support of that designation it came with shift paddles on the steering wheel. The company also claimed that the gearing and shift points had been optimized to give strong acceleration up to 100km/h (62mph).

All the engines in the 2013 Z4 range now met the EU6 emissions regulations that were due to be enforced for all new cars sold in Europe from September 2015. In pursuit of better fuel economy and lower overall emissions, all Z4s with manual gearboxes now came with an Automatic Stop-Start system as standard, which shut the engine off when the car was stationary (for example, waiting at traffic lights) and immediately restarted it once the clutch pedal was operated. Surprisingly, though, the 2013 models brought no changes to the 'chassis', even though the handling of the more powerful models had been questioned by a number

THE SECOND GENERATION Z4 – THE E89 MODELS

of commentators and aftermarket specialists had seen fit to develop improvements.

Nor were there any changes to the body sheet metal, and the only reliably quick way of recognizing one of the facelifted models was by the LED headlights. These now had a white 'eyebrow' similar to that seen on other BMW models of the time, with white LED corona rings as well. Depending on the colour of the paintwork, the new LED side repeater indicators let into the front apron just ahead of the wheel arch could also be seen. The central air vents now came with high-gloss black surrounds on all models, and there were redesigned tail lights as well. Inevitably, a couple of new alloy wheel designs were introduced to help freshen the Z4's appearance, while a new option followed the trend for two-tone paintwork. The 2013 cars could be had with a contrasting colour for the folding roof, which could be ordered in non-metallic black or Glacier Silver metallic.

Changes to the cabin interior were also limited, although better-quality materials for the control panel and its buttons and switches were welcome. Kansas leather remained standard on all except the 18i and 20i models, which had Panama cloth upholstery, and of course Extended Leather remained available too. The sDrive28i models gained an automatically dimming rear-view mirror as standard, and there was also a new wood trim option across the range that was called (rather clumsily) Exquisite Fineline Anthracite. Other changes were to the design package options.

A Pure Traction Design package was introduced in place of the earlier Design Pure Impulse package. Central to the new package were a unique Metal Weave interior trim, a Piano Black centre console surround and door handle inserts, and an Anthracite headlining. The seats were Sport types upholstered in black leather and alcantara, with orange highlights; the door inserts and the bottom of the instrument panel were in orange or black alcantara. All this was normally combined with special Valencia Orange paintwork and a contrasting Black folding roof. Other exterior colours could be ordered with the package, but the range of choices was limited by what went with the orange interior highlights.

More expensive than the Pure Traction Design package was another new option called the Pure Fusion Design package. Intended to go with Sparkling Brown metallic paint, it could also be ordered with other colours from the standard catalogue. Its unique features were Ivory White Nappa leather with high-gloss Fineline brown wood trim, Sport seats and an Anthracite headlining.

Two-Seater Future

At the time of writing, in autumn 2016, a replacement model for the E89 Z4 model was still anticipated. Some commentators had doubts about whether BMW would really build a new two-seater in view of the decline in sales, which for the E89 had peaked in 2010 and had been falling ever since. BMW's chief executive officer, Harald Krueger, was reported as answering a direct question about the viability of an E89 two-seater replacement by saying, 'We will occupy the segment once more. It's not big, but it's important for the strength of the brand.'

Rumours abounded. One strong possibility was that BMW planned to offset development costs of the replacement model by developing it as a joint project with Toyota, who would build their new Supra model on the same platform. Another was that the new car would be built by Magna-Steyr at Graz in Austria, after production of the Mini Paceman and Mini Countryman ended there.

One way or another, it seemed likely that there would be a future for BMW's 'affordable' two-seaters – and that the E89 models would gradually attain the status as modern classics that their E36/7, E85 and E86 forerunners already enjoyed.

Z4 PRODUCTION FIGURES, E89 MODELS

The figures relate to model years.

2009	22,761
2010	24,575
2011	18,809
2012	15,249
2013	12,866
2014	10,802

Production continued at the time of writing.

Z4 SPECIFICATIONS, E89 MODELS

Engines

2.0-litre (sDrive18i)
Type N20B20 4-cylinder petrol
1997cc (84 x 90.1mm)
Twin ohc, chain-driven
4v per cylinder
Double-VANOS variable valve timing and Valvetronic variable valve lift
Five-bearing crankshaft
Compression ratio 10.0:1
Bosch engine management system with direct fuel injection (GDI)
Twin-scroll turbocharger
Three-way catalytic converter standard
156PS (154bhp) at 5,000rpm
240Nm (177lb ft) from 1,250–4,400rpm

2.0-litre (sDrive20i)
Type N20B20 4-cylinder petrol
1997cc (84 x 90.1mm)
Twin ohc, chain-driven
4v per cylinder
Double-VANOS variable valve timing and Valvetronic variable valve lift
Five-bearing crankshaft
Compression ratio 10.0:1
Bosch engine management system with direct fuel injection (GDI)
Twin-scroll turbocharger
Three-way catalytic converter standard
184PS (181bhp) from 5,000–6,250rpm
270Nm (199lb ft) from 1,250–4,500rpm

2.0-litre (sDrive28i)
Type N20B20 4-cylinder petrol
1997cc (84 x 90.1mm)
Twin ohc, chain-driven
4v per cylinder
Double-VANOS variable valve timing and Valvetronic variable valve lift
Five-bearing crankshaft
Compression ratio 11.0:1
Bosch engine management system with direct fuel injection (GDI)
Twin-scroll turbocharger
Three-way catalytic converter standard
245PS (241bhp) from 5,000–6,500rpm
350Nm (258lb ft) from 1,250–4,800rpm

2.5-litre (sDrive23i)
Type N52B25 6-cylinder petrol
2497cc (82 x 78.8mm)
Twin ohc, chain-driven
4v per cylinder
Double-VANOS variable valve timing, Valvetronic and DISA
Seven-bearing crankshaft
Compression ratio 11.0:1
Siemens MSV70 engine management system
Three-way catalytic converter standard
204PS (201bhp) at 6,400rpm
250Nm (184lb ft) from 2,750–4,250rpm

3.0-litre (sDrive30i)
Type N52B30 6-cylinder petrol
2996cc (85 x 88mm)
Twin ohc, chain-driven
4v per cylinder
Double-VANOS variable valve timing
Seven-bearing crankshaft
Compression ratio 10.7:1
Siemens engine management system
Three-way catalytic converter standard
258PS (255bhp) at 6,600rpm
310Nm (229lb ft) at 2,600rpm

3.0-litre (sDrive35i)
Type N54B30 6-cylinder petrol
2979cc (84 x 89.6mm)

(continued overleaf...)

THE SECOND GENERATION Z4 – THE E89 MODELS

(continued from previous page)

Twin ohc, chain-driven
4v per cylinder
Double-VANOS variable valve timing
Seven-bearing crankshaft
Compression ratio 10.2:1
Siemens MSD80 engine management system
Twin Mitsubishi TD03-10TK3 turbochargers
Three-way catalytic converter standard
306PS (302bhp) at 5,800rpm
400Nm (295lb ft) from 1,300–5,000rpm

3.0-litre (sDrive35is)
Type N54B30TO 6-cylinder petrol
2979cc (84 × 89.6mm)
Twin ohc, chain-driven
4v per cylinder
Double-VANOS variable valve timing
Seven-bearing crankshaft
Compression ratio 10.2:1
Siemens engine management system
Twin turbochargers
Three-way catalytic converter standard
340PS (335bhp) at 5,800rpm
450Nm (332lb ft) from 1,400–4,500rpm
Transient overboost feature allows 500Nm (370lb ft) from 1,500–4,500rpm for brief periods

Transmission
Six-speed ZF manual gearbox standard
  Ratios 3.683:1, 2.062:1, 1.313:1, 1.00:1, 0.809:1, 0.677:1
Six-speed ZF automatic gearbox optional 2008–2013
  Ratios 2.40:1, 1.47:1, 1.00:1, 0.72:1
Eight-speed ZF automatic gearbox optional 2013 onwards
  Ratios 4.17:1, 2.34:1, 1.52:1, 1.14:1, 0.87:1, 0.69:1, 0.667:1
Seven-speed DCT standard on sDrive35is
  Ratios 4.78:1, 3.06:1, 2.15:1, 1.68:1, 1.39:1, 1.20:1, 1.00:1

Axle ratio
3.08:1   sDrive28i manual
2.56:1   sDrive35i and 35is

Suspension, steering and brakes
Front suspension with MacPherson struts and lower wishbones
Rear suspension with MacPherson struts and lower wishbones (Adaptive M Suspension optional)
Rack-and-pinion steering with 14.2:1 ratio and standard electric power assistance
Ventilated disc brakes all round, with twin hydraulic circuits and ABS

Dimensions
Overall length	4,239mm (166.9in)
Overall width	1,790mm (70.5in)
Overall height	1,291mm (50.8)
Wheelbase	2,495mm (98.2in)
Front track	1,511mm (59.5in)
Rear track	1,560mm (61.4in)

Wheels and tyres
8J × 17 alloy wheels, with 225/45 R 17 tyres
8J × 18 alloy wheels, with 225/40 R 18 tyres
8J × 19 alloy wheels, with 225/35 R19 tyres

Unladen weights
sDrive18i	1,395kg (3,075lb)
sDrive20i	1,395kg (3,075lb)
sDrive23i	1,405kg (3,097lb)
sDrive28i	1,400kg (3,086lb)
sDrive30i	1,415kg (3,119lb)
sDrive35i	1,505kg (3,318lb)
sDrive35is	1,525kg (3,362lb)

Z4 PERFORMANCE FIGURES, E89 MODELS

sDrive18i	0–60mph	7.6sec
	Maximum	137mph (220km/h)
sDrive20i	0–60mph	6.6sec
	Maximum	142mph (228km/h)
sDrive23i	0–60mph	6.3sec
	Maximum	150mph (242km/h)
sDrive28i	0–60mph	5.5sec
	Maximum	155mph (250km/h) (limited)
sDrive30i	0–60mph	5.8sec
	Maximum	155mph (250km/h) (limited)
sDrive35i	0–60mph	5.0sec (quoted as 5.2sec from 2013)
	Maximum	155mph (250km/h) (limited)
sDrive35is	0–60mph	4.6sec
	Maximum	155mph (250km/h) (limited)

CHAPTER NINE

A Z3 AND Z4 BUYER'S GUIDE

THE Z3 MODELS

The Z3 is a relatively simple car that is generally robust and trouble-free as long as it is looked after properly. However, genuine BMW parts and dealer servicing are expensive, and many owners have tried to reduce costs by buying aftermarket parts and finding cheaper servicing options. So a comprehensive service record helps to assess how a car has been treated. Few Z3s will have been serviced by BMW dealers all their lives, but invoices and servicing stamps from a well-regarded independent specialist are just as good a sign that a car has been properly maintained.

The choice of models is really very straightforward. Most Z3s were Roadsters, and the cars are probably best enjoyed in that form, but the alternative Coupé brings a stiffer bodyshell that can make drivers feel slightly more confident in the car's abilities. After the choice of body style, the only major decision is what engine to have – and that is especially important because the engine is fundamental to the driving character of a Z3.

Engines and Gearboxes

The 4-cylinder 1.8-litre and 1.9-litre engines give adequate performance, but certainly do not emphasize the Z3's sporting side. The soundtrack that accompanies them is surprisingly satisfying, with an aggressive snarl under hard acceleration. Up to about 100mph, they are generally as fast as most contemporary hatchbacks with similar engine power, but they will not impress hardcore sporting drivers.

For those who swore by BMW's smooth sixes, the 2.0-litre engine available after 1999 made the cheapest Z3 a much more attractive car, adding both refinement and performance. However, the 2.2-litre and 2.3-litre 6-cylinder cars are better compromises, with a good blend of performance and economy. Real performance and sports car qualities come with the 2.8-litre engines, which are smooth sixes in the best BMW tradition and deliver plenty of torque for acceleration. Fuel economy is also surprisingly good unless the engine is used very hard. The post-September 1998 engines with Double-VANOS have better power delivery characteristics. The later 3.0-litre engines are better still and, realistically, the best of the lot – unless you are prepared to go for an M car.

It is worth saying at the outset that the M cars are not the best choice for everybody. Even though the engines are pretty well beyond reproach in the performance and soundtrack departments, they are not best suited to short-distance commuting or to a lot of urban work. They can take plenty of hard use, but they do need careful servicing to keep them in top condition, and proper maintenance can be expensive.

The S50 and US-model S52 engines are rawer and harder than the later S54 type, seem to have less mid-range urge, and need to be revved harder to deliver their best. The later engine's drive-by-wire throttle gives smoother power delivery, which can make it more relaxing to drive in everyday conditions.

Wear in the VANOS system is a known weakness of the S50 and S52 engines; the later S54 types have less trouble with this. A grating sound from the front of the engine suggests VANOS trouble, as does an engine that feels down on power or runs roughly. All VANOS engines can rattle from cold until the oil has circulated fully. Other M engine weaknesses include the exhaust manifold, which can crack, and misfires caused by faulty coil packs. A ticking sound from the top end at low engine speeds suggests that the valve

A Z3 AND Z4 BUYER'S GUIDE

This publicity picture of a Z3 Roadster captures very well the thrill element of motoring in an open two-seater car.

clearances are adrift; putting these right is a bigger job than it sounds, although any competent specialist can deal with it.

Water pumps, radiators and expansion tanks on all Z3 engines can develop leaks, so keep an eye on the engine temperature gauge when test-driving a car. The viscous couplings in cooling fans can also fail after 80,000 miles (130,000km) or so, and this can be another cause of overheating. All Z3s come with BMW's service interval indicator, which uses red lights to indicate that a service is due. Typical service intervals on all but the M derivatives are likely to be around 15,000 miles (25,000km) – but a lot depends on the way the car is driven. For M cars, services may be twice as frequent.

Five-speed manual gearboxes were standard equipment, and have a nice sporty shift action that suits the nature of the Z3 well. The automatics – four-speed on earlier cars and five-speeds with AGS after mid-2000 – do reduce acceleration and are therefore not a choice favoured by sporting drivers. On the M cars, a rattle at idle after a hard drive is not uncommon, but should normally not be a cause for concern.

Bodywork and Structure

The Z3 is certainly not a delicate flower that needs to be pampered, and its all-steel structure and good build quality easily absorb demanding everyday use. There should be no significant corrosion, so if there are large areas of rust on a car, suspect poorly repaired crash damage or some other mishap such as flood damage.

The extreme nose of the car is invisible from the driving seat, and as a result that nose often receives minor parking damage. The bonnet may also rub against the front bumper

■ A Z3 AND Z4 BUYER'S GUIDE

'Some shapes are beautiful, others are convincing. A perfect shape is both.' BMW publicity allowed no doubts about the styling of the Z3, although not every onlooker was convinced.

'If you've found your own style, you don't need compromises.' BMW publicity argues here in favour of the uncompromising shape of the Z3 Coupé.

Boot size is an important factor; would a Z3's boot be large enough for everything you want to carry?

at its leading edge, exposing bare metal. This is not a particular problem – but if this kind of damage has not been repaired, it suggests the car has not been cared for very well. Reversing needs care in a Z3, so look out for scuffing on the rear apron.

More worrying is that the high torque outputs of the bigger-engined Z3s can overstress the rear subframe mountings. Look carefully in and underneath the boot for signs of weld failures and for cracks; repairs may be tricky and expensive. On the M models, the boot floor can actually tear around the differential mounting – a problem that becomes most obvious as a creaking noise from the back of the car. Beware, too, of grounding damage to the underside of the fuel tank; repair involves removing the tank, and the suspension has to be dropped clear of the car first.

Soft Tops, Hardtops and Fixed Roofs

On Roadsters, always check that the soft top raises and lowers satisfactorily; it is powered electrically on later cars. The roof should be firmly attached to its frame, and not torn, scuffed or faded. With the roof erect, check the well that it folds into for any damage that is otherwise invisible. Take a good look at the way the fabric sits on the windscreen header rail and above the windows, too; these are favourite areas for leaks.

Make sure, too, that the plastic rear screen is in good condition. Note that the stitching that attaches the zip can fail, and replacement is best left to a professional. Aftermarket soft tops are available, and can be considerably cheaper than the genuine BMW item. The optional hardtop for the Roadster was never very common, and needs a fitting kit installed on the car's body. So never buy a second-hand hardtop unless it comes with such a kit or there is one on your Z3. The attractive aftermarket Wiesmann hardtop was even rarer, and uses a different fitting kit.

On Coupés, a sunroof was an extra-cost option, even on the M models. It does not normally give trouble, but there is always merit in checking that it opens and closes properly and smoothly. The rear screen can also delaminate, and the sign of this is a milky discoloration around the edges. If the rear wiper fails to operate, the most likely cause is a broken power wire to the motor.

On both body types, make sure that the electric windows operate smoothly, too. If their operation is jerky or erratic, the lift mechanism may need to be re-greased. If they have failed altogether, a more careful examination is needed to determine the cause.

Interior

The Z3's cabin is not spacious, so taller people often find the driving position cramped. Some owners have fitted aftermarket seats to gain more headroom and improve comfort, and the sports seats fitted as standard to the M models are generally more supportive than those in the mainstream cars.

Upholstery, whether cloth or leather, is hard-wearing. Seat mounting bushes can become compressed, allowing the seats to move under acceleration or braking. Elements of the plastic trim can rub together and cause irritating squeaks that are hard to trace; in some areas the brittle plastic can even crack or break. A well-known problem area is the glovebox, which has a heavy lid that eventually sags and then rattles when the car goes over bumps.

Electrics in general are a well-known weakness, so it is worth checking carefully on a car offered for sale whether everything works as it should. The electric window lifts (see above) and central locking system can fail, and so can the electric seat adjustment mechanism; any hesitation in these electrical components is a sign that failure is not far away.

Steering, Suspension, Wheels and Tyres

All Z3s handle very securely, with a slight tendency to understeer that blends smoothly into a neutral feel as the power is applied. These are not by any means tail-happy sports cars, although ultimate grip is compromised by the semi-trailing arm rear suspension, and the bigger the engine, the clearer that suspension's limitations become.

However, the whole suspension system is generally long-lived and reliable, as well as cheap because it shares parts with the 3 Series cars. Dampers normally last for up to 80,000 miles (130,000km) or so. At the front, the lower ball joints and the inner bushes on the wishbones can wear in exactly the same way as they do on the saloons. Rattles from the rear may come from worn rear subframe mountings or from the top damper mountings.

Always check the electrical equipment on a Z3. Power seat switches can fail if the seat has been left in one position for a long time.

Worn seats result from the relatively small cockpit space. Excessive wear might be a good bargaining point when buying.

Another useful bargaining point may be the condition of the alloy wheels. They can of course be refurbished for a fraction of the cost of new ones.

Some genuinely useful accessories were available from BMW, such as this boot rack for carrying extra luggage.

■ A Z3 AND Z4 BUYER'S GUIDE

Another BMW accessory was the Speedster Cover, designed purely for looks.

Twin tailpipes were a distinguishing feature of the 6-cylinder Z3s.

A Z3 AND Z4 BUYER'S GUIDE

Inevitably, some owners have fitted modified suspension, which is not a problem in itself but there are properly engineered conversions and others which consist of little more than shorter springs that give a hard ride.

The standard brakes are more than adequate for road use. On the mainstream Z3s, discs can be expected to last for around 30,000–40,000 miles (50,000–65,000km). On the M cars, the brakes are of course the more powerful 'floating' or two-piece discs that were used on the E36 M3; they are also more expensive to replace than the discs on the mainstream cars.

Scuffed and kerbed alloy wheels always make a car look down-at-heel, but can usually be refurbished to as-new condition by specialists for very much less than the cost of new wheels. Low-profile tyres inevitably make kerbing damage more likely, and owners of early Roadsters with steel wheels should probably be grateful that their cars are unlikely to need replacement wheels – a repaint will make them look like new again.

Tyre life depends on the way the car is driven. Front tyres will typically last for 30,000 miles (50,000km) apiece, and rear ones for rather less – perhaps 20,000 miles (32,000km) or so. On hard-used M cars, tyre life may well be shorter. Wide, low-profile tyres are always likely to be noisy, and always check that the space-saver emergency spare is in its place on a car offered for sale.

THE E85 AND E86 Z4 MODELS

One of the strange things about the E85 and E86 Z4 models has always been that their owners love them even though the motoring media, on the whole, has been quite negative about them. Clearly, the cars often did not meet the expectations of motoring writers, but equally clearly they did meet the expectations of those who actually bought them. This rather suggests that BMW was right on target commercially with what it was doing, while the mismatch lay between the expectations of writers and Z4 buyers.

The good news is that the E85 and E86 models have so far proved to be robust, reliable cars with few major weaknesses. So the main questions when buying one are likely to centre on specification. There are, though, some common problems to bear in mind.

Engines and Gearboxes

There is no shortage of engine options for these cars, from the entry-level 2.0-litre 4-cylinder to the fire-breathing 3.2-litre 6-cylinder in the Z4 M models. BMW traditionalists tend to insist on a 6-cylinder, but many owners find the 2.0-litre 4-cylinder smoother than the smaller sixes, and ultimately more enjoyable to use. In particular, the 2.2-litre

The E85 Z4 always looked good from low angles, but its shape divided opinions quite sharply.

■ A Z3 AND Z4 BUYER'S GUIDE

The E85's cockpit was an interesting mix of modern ideas with roadster cues from the past.

The **Z4 M** dashboard added more luxury features as well as a more sporting air.

An open road and a sunny day: this is what owning a BMW roadster of any kind is all about.

6-cylinder has sometimes been criticized for combining relatively poor fuel economy with inadequate performance, which would make it the worst choice of them all.

Rough running and misfires on any of these engines might well be caused by faulty coil packs or sensors. Some owners have reported premature water pump wear and high oil consumption on the M54 6-cylinders. On the S54 engines, the VANOS system sometimes gives trouble, but much less so than on earlier engines with the system. Early N52 engines sometimes 'tick' noticeably when the hydraulic lifters are not getting enough oil, and BMW issued a technical bulletin about this. A redesigned cylinder head in 2008 solved the problem.

Most E85 and E86 models have the six-speed manual gearbox, which tends to require the driver to make positive changes. It is fine for open-road driving, but can feel positively obstructive in town traffic. Rattles at idle are unfortunately quite normal. Problems are associated with the first-to-second gear change, which sometimes produces grinding noises – especially in the Z4 M models. Online forums have suggested various cures, from changing the gearbox fluid to removing the Clutch Delay Valve (CDV).

This is the 6-cylinder engine in an early Z4; all engines in the E85 and E86 models were concealed under plastic cosmetic covers.

For a car that is to be used mostly in town traffic, an automatic gearbox is the best choice. As for the fairly rare SMG, it is not a gearbox for every driver: try before you buy.

Bodywork and Structure

The E85 and E86 models came with a twelve-year anti-corrosion warranty, so BMW were clearly confident that they were on top of that problem. As a result, any sign of corrosion on a Z4 should be treated with suspicion. It usually means that the car has been damaged in an accident and repaired cheaply.

So saying, there may be plenty of scratches on the bumper valances and even the rear wheel arches. Visibility for reversing is not good, so this is perhaps excusable, but big gouges out of the rear bumper are to be avoided because of the cost of putting them right. At the front, the long nose also makes visibility tricky, and few cars will have escaped parking scrapes completely. There is likely to be a rash of stone chips at the front, too.

The bonnet is made of aluminium, and its large flat expanse means that dents show up clearly. It is harder to knock dents out of aluminium than out of steel, so be prepared for larger repair bills if there is bonnet damage. Some cars will have minor damage around the twin kidney grilles, too, and this can be hard to put right effectively. Worth knowing is that the bonnet release can stick; the bonnet can usually be opened if somebody pushes down on it (but not too hard) while you pull the release lever, and then the cure is to lubricate the mechanism.

Even though the headlights do have vents, water that gets into the units can sometimes be trapped there. Fitting new headlight covers with new seals (not expensive) is probably the best solution unless you have infinite patience and time to find where the water is getting in. Another, somewhat bizarre, fault in this area is that the headlight washer nozzle covers have been known to part company with the car at speed.

On all cars, check the condition of the braces between the bulkhead and the tops of the suspension struts. These are present to prevent scuttle shake, but if a car has been used hard they can crack near the strut tops. Repairs are likely to be expensive – and of course this sort of damage

A Z3 AND Z4 BUYER'S GUIDE

TOP AND BOTTOM: The pop-up screen on the E85 dashboard had several uses. These pictures show it providing navigation guidance and a sound read-out for the optional Hi-Fi Professional sound system.

183

A Z3 AND Z4 BUYER'S GUIDE

Extra width in the cockpit, easily visible in this picture, makes the E85 Z4 more comfortable than the earlier Z3.

may suggest that hard use has caused problems elsewhere on the car.

Sundry other faults to look out for when buying a car include wiper blades that park incorrectly or wipers that do not work at all (grease building up in the motor is the probable cause); door handles that stick in the open position (lubrication usually cures this, although a new handle is sometimes needed); and petrol filler caps that fall off their clips.

Soft Tops, Hardtops and Fixed Roofs

The choice between E85 Roadster and E86 Coupé is of course fundamental – and irreversible. So it is important to determine which body style you really want. The Coupé is available with a much more restricted range of engine options, which may be a consideration.

There is nothing special to say about the Coupé roof. As for the Roadster's optional hardtop, it is a welcome accessory but does demand careful storage when not in use. However, the folding roof is generally considered to be one of the major problem areas in the Roadster.

On the outside, check that the hood is not coming away from the edges of the glass rear screen and that there has been no damage to the elements of that heated rear window. On the inside, make sure the hood lining is not hanging down. Most important is to make sure that the power-operated soft top actually goes up and down without difficulty, because water can get into the electric motor that powers the hydraulic system and can cause it to fail. If the hood is noticeably slow to operate, motor failure is probably imminent.

What happens is that the drain holes in the hood well can become blocked, so allowing water running off the hood to build up. It is then absorbed by the padding and trim around the motor, and eventually enters the motor itself. On early Z4s, the problem was made worse by a plastic tray around the motor that also collected water. When test-driving a car, listen carefully for the sound of water sloshing about in the hood well – a sure sign that the drain holes are blocked. The only cure for a failed motor is replacement, and to get access to the motor the hood has to be removed first. A less expensive problem associated with the hood is failure of one or more of the microswitches that ensure correct operation.

Interior

You sit deep within the Z4 rather than perching on it as in the Z3, and the interior ergonomics are excellent. On the downside, the boot is small, so careful packing and soft bags are needed for weekends away.

Generally speaking, the Z4's cabin is well made and durable, but there are likely to be plenty of rattles and creaks from the trim, especially on the less rigid Roadster models. Favourite sources of noise are the outer edges of seats where the leather upholstery touches the plastic seat frames; the glovebox; the lower plastic section of the instrument panel; the trim below the air conditioning controls; the area around the cupholders; the lid of the centre console stowage box; the speaker grilles behind the seats; and the interior light. Cars with the bigger wheel and stiffer suspension options suffer most. Owners say that felt tape and perseverance can cure most noises – but tracing those noises can be time-consuming and frustrating.

Another source of rattles can be the door windows. Sometimes, tightening a screw on the lower part of the door cures this. However, on early cars the window glass can actually come away from its regulator and even drop into the door cavity. This problem was common enough for BMW to issue a service bulletin about it. If the car is fitted with a folding navigation screen, make sure that this is not sticking in either the open or shut position; there appears to be no cure except replacement. Worth testing (despite the difficulty of doing so) are the automatic rain-sensing wipers, if they are fitted – and an alarm that goes off unexpectedly will indicate a faulty bonnet alarm switch or possibly a battery that is on its last legs (the voltage drop triggers the alarm).

Steering, Suspension, Wheels and Tyres

If the steering feels sticky in hot weather, beware: this is a fault that has to be cured by fitting a new steering column assembly. Wear in the suspension control arms and ball joints is hard to diagnose while driving because of the generally numb feel of the electric power steering, but a vibration through the steering wheel suggests that a closer look at these components is worthwhile.

The standard suspension is perfectly adequate for most owners, and only hardcore enthusiasts really need the stiffer options. Listen for problems, especially over rough surfaces. If there are knocks from the front end, it may be time to

The combination of BMW logo and side repeater indicator was common to all E85 and E86 models – but only the Z4 M had the M badge as well.

tighten the bolts holding the strut tower braces. A rattle from behind could be caused by a broken spring, but the rubber bushes on the rear damper mounts also wear and cause noises. Under the car, it is wise to check the anti-roll bar mounting rubbers, too.

All these cars were supplied with run-flat tyres when new. Modern types are better than the early ones, but owners generally agree that they give a more lumpy ride than traditional tyres, especially with the larger wheel sizes and the Sport suspension. The tyres can also become noisy and cause excessive tramlining. Many E85 and E86 owners have switched to traditional tyres at replacement time, but as there is no space to carry a spare wheel in the Z4, it is important to carry a can of emergency repair foam in the boot as well.

Note, too, that the TPMS valves fitted with run-flat tyres are prone to failure because of electrolytic action between the valve caps and the valve stems. A simple preventative measure is to use plastic valve caps instead of the standard metal ones. As for the wheels, always check for kerbing damage, and be aware that even the most attractive wheels can look shabby if paint and lacquer finishes start to come off.

THE E89 Z4 MODELS

BMW's third-generation 'affordable' roadster was still in production as this book went to press, and even the earliest cars were not really old enough to have revealed what the E89's long-term trouble areas might be. Many E89 Z4s were used as second cars from new, with the result that they have reached or will reach the second-hand and enthusiast markets with surprisingly low mileages.

An important point to remember is that the E89 was deliberately designed as a comfortable roadster, and not in the mould of the traditional, wind-in-the-hair sports car. In that respect, it is more different from the Z3s and earlier Z4s than might appear at first sight. However, it would be wrong to get the idea that this is not a proper sports car. Its standard DDC system allows the car to be used harder when the mood takes the driver, and BMW also offered several options – notably the Adaptable M Suspension – that tighten the car's responses at the expense of ride comfort. There is a hardcore sports car to be had in the E89 if that is what you want: the key thing is to understand which options are necessary to provide it.

Hardcore or not, the retractable hardtop of the E89 Z4 is a massive benefit. It eliminates the main problems associated with a traditional fabric soft top (such as damage and wear to the fabric, the struggle of opening or closing the roof manually, and – mostly – leaks). It also means there is no need to make the irreversible choice between roadster and coupé versions of the car that is necessary with the Z3 and first-generation Z4 models. There are compromises, of course, and boot space is one of them, but most owners find these acceptable for the greater convenience that this modern roof system brings.

On the whole, owners report that the E89 Z4 is easy to live with on a day-to-day basis. It is comfortable enough, big enough and convenient enough to work as everyday transport for one person or two, and yet its sporting side is always available to liven up a dull day. Despite early criticism that the E89 roadster was simply a soft sports car, it seems that BMW caught the needs and moods of its potential customers rather well.

Engines and Gearboxes

The engine in an E89 is central to the car's character, as it is in the other BMW two-seat models. This is the only one of the cars covered in this book which does not have an M derivative, and such is the cachet attached to the coveted M cars that this fact alone might discourage some buyers from even considering it as a purchase. Undeniably, there is a special character about the cars from BMW's M division.

However, BMW probably got it right again when they claimed that there was no need for an M variant of the

The great advance of the E89 Z4 models was a folding roof, which meant that the car could be used like a coupé with the roof closed . . .

A Z3 AND Z4 BUYER'S GUIDE

...while the roof could be rapidly lowered if the sun came out and the road was right for an enjoyable drive.

E89 because the sDrive35i (and later 35is) were quite fast enough. A look at the performance figures for these cars is helpful. Several models are capable of reaching 155mph (250km/h) – the speed to which even the M cars have traditionally been limited) – and the 0–60mph acceleration times of the quicker models do make good comparison with the M derivatives of the earlier two-seaters. An E89 sDrive35is can reach 60mph from rest in 4.6sec – faster than an E85 or E86 Z4 M (4.7sec) or a Z3 M Roadster or Coupé (5.2sec in their faster European versions).

Unlike earlier models, the designations given to the E89 cars do not necessarily reflect the engine size, or do so only approximately. All the early models had 6-cylinder engines, for which BMW has been justly famous, and there is no doubt that these provide a very satisfying soundtrack, especially with the roof open. However, the need to reduce exhaust emissions and fuel consumption persuaded the company to downsize to turbocharged 4-cylinders for the entry-level and mid-range cars from 2012. The 245PS (241bhp) from the engine of an sDrive28i is certainly not to be sniffed at, and even an sDrive18i can reach 100km/h (62mph) from rest in a respectable 7.9sec. In performance terms, then, the 4-cylinder models live up to the BMW name. It is only for their less interesting-sounding engine notes that they merit some criticism – and even then they sound much more sporty when pressed hard.

So which is the best engine to have? It depends very much on what you want from the car. If an E89 is the choice because it offers open-air versatility and performance is not a big issue, an sDrive18i will be perfectly adequate. Some owners argue that an early sDrive30i is the best choice, and some press reports have suggested that the sDrive35i and sDrive35is are too powerful for their chassis. Meanwhile, the lighter 4-cylinder engines can give sharper turn-in characteristics than the 6-cylinders. The best solution is to try several different cars and see which one suits you best.

The standard six-speed gearbox is sporty enough for most users, and easy enough to use for those less interested in sporty driving. A few cars (and all sDrive35is models) have the DCT transmission, which has its own devotees and can shave tenths of seconds off acceleration times thanks to its lighting-fast changes. However, this is definitely for hardcore drivers only; most drivers who enjoy the occasional bout of quick driving will be quite happy without it. And, of course, not every E89 will be bought for its driving dynamics; in particular, if the car is to spend most of its life in town traffic, then the optional automatic gearbox is the best choice. Bear in mind, though, that automatics are rarer than manuals (except in the USA) and are likely to be more expensive.

Worth knowing is that there have been some fuel system issues with the twin-turbocharged engines in the sDrive35i and sDrive35is. There have been problems with the low-pressure fuel pump (listen for a loud hum from the fuel tank area) and, more commonly, with the high-pressure pump. Symptoms include the engine taking a long time to start; the engine warning light on the dash may also illuminate. Some owners have also encountered problems with injectors – but many problems of this sort will have been put right by BMW under warranty.

■ A Z3 AND Z4 BUYER'S GUIDE

Cosmetic engine covers featured on the E89 models too . . . and it takes a good knowledge of the different types even to work out what sort of engine this is!

Somehow, the model names for the E89 Z4 range always seemed too long and complicated.

Bodywork and Structure

Build quality of the E89 models has always been up to BMW's high standards, so any bodywork problems deserve investigation. Uneven shut lines around doors or boot, and questionable panel gaps elsewhere, strongly suggest that the car has been repaired inexpertly after an accident. Overspray on normally hidden areas of the car point to repairs, and paint problems generally should ring alarm bells. There will be stone chips around the nose of the car, and the more there are, the more fun previous owners had driving it! However, owners who look after their cars touch-in paint chips to prevent them developing into corrosion; owners who neglect their cars do not. Draw your own conclusions about the way the car has been treated from what you see.

Over time, a mechanism as complex as that of the retractable hardtop will inevitably develop rattles and vibrations. So will other areas of the car, and owners have flagged up noises from the seats and the rear deck. Many of these noises can be irritating, and also very time-consuming to trace. It is always worth checking the online forums relating to the E89 cars to see how other owners have dealt with them – but there is rarely such a thing as a permanent cure!

The E89 dashboard was remarkably sophisticated, reflecting the careful sophistication of this third 'affordable' roadster from BMW. Once again, the pop-up dashboard screen is here being used for navigation . . .

Interior

Worth knowing when looking for a car to buy is that the manual seat adjustment can be difficult to use, so the optional electric adjustment (standard on some models) is well worth having. If examining a car which has it, check that all the seat motors actually work. The more 'toys' there are on the car, the more there is to go wrong, so it is wise to check everything.

Not everybody finds the iDrive system easy to use (although it is much improved over its original incarnation in the 7 Series BMWs). And an interesting battery-drain problem can be linked to the Bluetooth system. If the system is set to search for the owner's mobile phone, it will continue to use battery power to do so even when the owner has gone on holiday unless the car has been locked and all the electrical systems have been shut down.

. . . and in this case for finding nearby attractions.
WIKIMEDIA/PLEIN

■ A Z3 AND Z4 BUYER'S GUIDE

Never mind what the neighbours think, or the hypercritical road-testers . . . there is nothing quite like having a BMW roadster parked on your drive.

Steering, Suspension, Wheels and Tyres

Not everybody likes the feel of the standard electric power-assisted steering, but there is no alternative to it. The 2013 model (LCI) and later cars have some improvements in this area, and it is worth trying both pre- and post-facelift cars for this reason.

The standard wheels on E89s have a 17in diameter, and 18in sizes are the most common alternatives. Some owners have reported that the ride deteriorates badly if the less common 19in wheels are fitted – and of course these bigger tyres are more expensive to replace when renewal becomes necessary. The M Sport suspension option is fine for those who want a hardcore sports car, but for others it gives a ride that is too firm.

As a matter of course, check alloy wheels for kerbing damage. There have also been instances of wheels cracking, possibly as a result of running over potholes.

INDEX

007 Bond Edition of Z3 34
328 Hommage 160
328 model 10
503 model 14
507 model 14, 29
100,000th Z3 41
100,000th Z4 98
250,000th Z3 roadster 64

AC Schnitzer, and Z4 (E85) 101
   and Z4 (E89) 159
AFM 12
AGS 59
Alpina, and Z4 101
Arnaout, Nadya 145
ASC 93, 119
ASC + T traction control 37
automatic dry braking 119

Bangle, Chris 27, 88, 145
Blasi, Juliane 145
BMW Individual, and Z3 40, 57
BMW Technik 19, 21, 22, 44
brake assist 149
brake energy regeneration 149
brake standby 119
business and professional ICE systems 119

Canadian special edition, M Roadster 77
CBC 119, 149
concept coupé, Z4 104, 108
coupé, Z3 44
   Z4 114

daytime running lights 152
DBC 119, 149
DDC 97, 119, 149
design and development, Z3 27

Z4 (E85) 89
Z4 (E89) 144
Dinan, and M derivatives of Z3 82
DISA 104, 112
Dixi 7
DSC 53, 80, 93, 119, 149
DTC 93, 119, 149

E36/7 code 27
E36/8 code 44
Edition Exclusive 122
Edition Sport 122
efficient dynamics 149, 159
engine codes 112
engines, Z3 27

fading compensation 119
features and options, 2006 Z4 118
Fiedler, Fritz 10
Fiji special edition (Z3) 46
first Z3s 33
first Z4s (E85) 94
folding roof 145

GoldenEye, and the Z3 32
GT3 derivative of Z4 155

Hamann hardtop for Z3 64
   and Z4 (E85) 103
   and Z4 (E89) 159
Hartge, and M derivatives of Z3 82
   and Z4 103, 134
hill-start assistant 149

individual editions, Z3 57
Infinitas, and Z4
Isetta 13

Keelmagen, Wolfgang 88, 108
Klanner, Martin 88

Krusche, Heinz 148

last Z3 63
last Z4 (E85/E86) 123
launch, Z3 32
Life Cycle Impulse (LCI), E89 167
Loof, Ernst 10, 12

M coupé 77
M roadster (Z3) 41
M roadster development 70
M roadster, for Europe 71
M roadster, for North America 74
M sport package (E89) 151
M44 engine 45
M52 engine 37, 45, 52, 57, 58
M54 engine 58
Mazda MX-5 (Miata) 20, 31
Michelotti, Giovanni 16
Mille Miglia 10
Mille Miglia concept coupé 139
Motorsport coupé (E86 Z4) 136
Motor sport and the E89 161

N20 engines 159
N46 engines 104
N52 engines 112, 149
Nagashima, Joji 27

options, E89 Z4 152
Orinoco special edition (Z3) 46

Paint options, 1996-1999 Z3 47
   2000–2002 Z3 65
   2003–2005 Z4 105
   2006–2008 Z4 124
   M coupé 84
   M roadster 83
   Z4 M Coupé and M Roadster 141
patents, for Z3 31

INDEX

performance figures, 1996–1999 Z3 49
  2000–2002 Z3 67
  2003–2005 Z4 107
  2006–2008 Z4 125
  M coupé and M roadster 87
  Z4 (E89) 171
press reactions, to initial Z3s 35
  to M Coupé 79
  to M Roadster 74
  to S54-engined Z3s 81
  to Z3 2.8 43
  to 1999 models 45
  to 2000 models 56
  to 2001 models 63
  to initial Z4s 98
  to 2006 Z4s 120
  to Z4 M Coupé 138
  to Z4 M Roadster 134
production changes, M Roadsters, 1997–2001 76
  M Roadsters and Coupés, 2001–2002 79
  Z4 M Coupés 135, 141
  Z4 M Roadsters 134, 140
production totals, mainstream Z3 68
  M coupé and M roadster 85
  Z4 (E85 and E86) 123
  Z4 (E89) 168

Quandt brothers 16

Regensburg factory 149
Reitzle, Wolfgang 44
Rennsport, and Z4 103
run-flat tyres 94

S50 engine 70
S52 engine 58, 70
S54 engine 79, 129
Sapphire Edition 61
sDrive 35is 155
sDrive name 150
Set-off Assistant 119
SMG 97, 101
South African M coupés 82
Spartanburg factory 23, 112
Specifications, 1996–1999 Z3 47
  2000–2002 Z3 65
  2003–2005 Z4 106
  2006–2008 Z4 125
  M Coupé and M Roadster 86
  Z4 (E89) 169
  Z4 M Coupé and M Roadster 143
Speedster cover 53
Sport Automatic 113
Sport Edition, Z3 61
Steptronic 97
stop/start system 149

Titanium Edition 61
twin-power turbo engine 159
tyre pressure monitoring system 151

UK introduction, Z3 33
upholstery options, M Roadster 83
  M Coupé 84
  Z4 M Coupé and M Roadster 142

Valvetronic 112
VANOS 73
Veritas 12
VINs for Z3 68
  for M Coupé and M Roadster 85
Von Falkenhausen, Alex 10, 12
Von Goertz, Albrecht 14

Warming, Anders 88
Wiesmann hardtop, for Z3 38

Z1 19
Z (meaning) 19
Z3 2.0, introduced 52
Z3 2.2i, introduced 58
Z3 2.3, introduced 45
Z3 2.8, introduced 37
Z3 3.0i, introduced 58
Z3, 1998 model-year 41
  1999 model-year 45
  2000 model-year 50
  2001 model-year 57
  2002 model-year 63
Z4, 2004 model-year 97
  2005 and 2006 model-years 104
  2007 and 2008 model-years 122
  2009 model-year (E89) 150
  2010 model-year 155
  2011 model-year 159
  2013 model-year 166
Z4 GTE (E89) 165
Z4 M Roadster 127
Zagato concepts 161